Anstey's Rights of L

Anstey's Rights of Light

and how to deal with them

Updated by Lance Harris

FOURTH EDITION

Published by RICS Business Services Limited
a wholly owned subsidiary of
The Royal Institution of Chartered Surveyors
under the RICS Books imprint
Surveyor Court
Westwood Business Park
Coventry CV4 8JE
UK

ISBN 978 1 84219 222 1
ISBN 1 84219 222 1 (prior to January 2007)

First edition November 1988
Second edition November 1992
Third edition January 1998

Illustrations by Michael Cromar

The royalties from the sale of this book go to the John Anstey Foundation, a charitable trust.

Typeset by Columns Design Ltd., Reading
Printed in Europe by the Alden Group, Oxford

Contents

Contents

Introduction
By Lance Harris

When I first joined Anstey Horne & Co as a Trainee
Building Surveyor in 1978, I had no concept of surveying
or the construction industry, let alone what rights of light
and party wall matters were all about. (This was before the
days when everyone took the easy option of a building
surveying degree.) Therefore, despite the fact that John
Anstey was by that time already a leading practitioner in
both fields, I was blissfully unaware of his elevated status
in the profession. However, anyone who was lucky enough
to have known him personally, or sensible enough to have
read his various books on rights of light, party walls and
boundary disputes, will know that he was fully aware of
his eminence, and will also understand that within a few
days of employment my ignorance was rectified in full!

John announced to me that he was 'the world's leading
expert', which one might consider a touch brash – but he
was. Over the years that I was fortunate enough to work
for and with him at Anstey Horne & Co – moving up
from teaboy to business partner – a little of my youthful
ignorance fell away and I began to appreciate his true
standing.

I was therefore very grateful, and not a little flattered,
when RICS Books invited me to produce this revised

edition of *Rights of Light and how to deal with them*. However, when I set about the task, I became immediately and uncomfortably conscious of how difficult it was to try to follow in John's footsteps. In my opinion, and that of many others, John's books have been nothing short of excellent: eminently readable, informative and truly representative of his style and character.

As very clearly stated in all of his books, they were intended as practical handbooks for surveyors and others with an interest in the subject, and not as definitive legal tomes. Indeed, it is worth repeating John's original disclaimer here, in which he noted that while he always gave his view of the law as carefully as he could, and made it clear when he was expressing a personal opinion, readers would be extremely foolish to rush off to court without taking careful legal and professional advice about their particular cases. He added that no book, and certainly not one meant to be a readable guide, could cover every eventuality. The same disclaimer naturally applies to this new edition.

For those both desirous of more detailed knowledge, and blessed with greater powers of concentration and stamina, I would point you to *Rights Of Light, The Modern Law*, published by Jordan Publishing Limited in 2000. This takes the form of a legal textbook on the subject of rights of light, and is written by Stephen Bickford-Smith and Andrew Francis (both eminent barristers who have come to specialise in the field). It includes a very helpful section on measurement and valuation of light by Elizabeth de Burgh Sidley, a building surveyor who, like me, has followed the potentially dangerous, but interesting and enjoyable path of rights of light consultancy.

I have tried to be true to John's approach (with regard to the law, opinions and in all other matters) in this revised edition – concentrating on the practical aspects, aiming for readability, and attempting to maintain the same level of entertainment value in terms of anecdotes. Much of John's advice and commentary obviously remain true today, and many of his quips and stories are likewise retained in this new edition. However, I have tried to weave into the text my thoughts on changes of significance or interest, and have added alternative views on certain aspects where I thought it appropriate.

In particular, Chapter 14, on planning aspects, has been entirely rewritten. All of the few good men and women in this field tend to refer to themselves, generically, as 'rights of light consultants'. However, in truth that description is only strictly correct as a reference to the legal – common law – aspects of the subject. Although it was always so, it is now increasingly the case that we consultants divide our time between the law, and daylight and sunlight issues arising out of the Town and Country Planning process. I have not attempted to assess the percentage of my professional time now committed to light in the planning sense, but suffice it to say that it is taking on increasing importance, and that this trend is unlikely to change in the near future. The third edition of this book included a chapter on the planning aspect, with an introduction to the Building Research Establishment (BRE) Guide 'Site Layout Planning for Daylight and Sunlight: A Guide to Good Practice'. I have simply expanded upon that previous chapter with my own views on the increasing importance of daylight and sunlight as part of the Town and Country Planning process.

My other contribution was intended to be an introduction to the implications arising out of the *Human Rights Act* 1998 and the long-awaited High Hedges Bill. As things transpired the High Hedges Bill never materialised, but certain aspects of the proposed bill were incorporated in the *Anti-social Behaviour Act* 2003 and I have therefore included a brief summary of the relevant parts. In truth, both topics are covered swiftly to reflect their relative unimportance in the context of the subject as a whole.

Additions, and the occasional difference of authorial opinion notwithstanding, in common with the other two updated books in this series (*Anstey's Boundary Disputes* and *Anstey's Party Walls*), my voice has been merged with that of John's throughout the text, in the hope that the reader will find the reading experience as seamless as possible.

Again in common with the other two books in this series, another note on the 'reading experience' is necessary here. More and more women are involved at all stages, and all levels, of rights to light problems, cases and consultancy. Again for ease of reading, this book, when speaking generically, uses the masculine form of address. It is to be understood though, that except where this would be entirely inappropriate, references to the masculine include the feminine.

When I attended my first interview at Anstey Horne, fresh from school, John criticised my hair (too long), the way I spoke, and my poor grasp of English grammar.

Despite my current commando-style haircut, I suspect that not much has changed in the other respects. However, I would have liked John to know how hard I now try to avoid split infinitives, and that I do understand the difference between 'affect' and 'effect'. I can only hope that with the assistance of the editors at RICS Books (in case he is still checking up on me), he would approve of my contribution to this new edition of his outstanding book.

Before finalising the drafting of this addition a new legal case has hit the streets and caused something of a stir in the rights of light field. I have therefore attempted to weave the impact and relevance of that case – *Midtown Limited v City of London Real Property Company Ltd*, 2005, into the general text of this revised edition and added a more detailed note to 'Some interesting cases' in the appendix.

John finished his original Introduction to the earlier editions of this book by noting that he was never more pleased than when he received a letter thanking him for his succinct and straightforward advice. It was his aim, and is mine for this new edition, to help you provide the same service to your clients. If you feel that the book has helped you to do so, then both the authors will have succeeded in their ambition.

What is a right to light?

A right to light is an easement: that is to say, it is a right acquired by one party (the dominant owner) over someone else's land. This latter person is called the servient owner.

There are surprisingly few natural rights in English law, and many people are mistakenly under the impression that certain rights exist which do not. There are, contrariwise, a surprising number of rights which can be acquired; John used to enjoy citing the unusual examples of being able to acquire a right to mix muck on a neighbour's land, or project one's bowsprit over his land. You may not be surprised to hear that Lance has not yet come across these examples in his professional career. However, there is also the better-known right to acquire a 'right to light' over a neighbour's land, with which this book is of course concerned.

What is an easement?

The definition above leads us on to another question, 'What exactly is an easement?'. The characteristics of an easement were set out in a 1956 case known as *Re Ellenborough Park*. They are as follows:

1. there must be a dominant and servient tenement;
2. an easement must accommodate the dominant tenement;

3. dominant and servient owners must be different persons; and
4. a right over land cannot amount to an easement, unless it is capable of forming the subject matter of a grant.

John would rightly refer readers to *Gale on the Law of Easements* (published by Sweet and Maxwell) for a detailed examination of these four characteristics, and had a favourite anecdote a propos the 14th edition of this work. He was attending a conference with Counsel, and had propounded a certain view of the law. When counsel asked where he had got that idea from, John replied: 'From Gale'. Counsel took a well-worn copy from his bookshelf, and started to flick through it, but John took it from him, saying that he could probably find the passage quicker than he. He did so, and handed it back to Counsel. The latter read the page and said: 'Well, I know I put my name to this volume, but ...'. John was never sure who was the more embarrassed – Counsel, because John had to point it out to him, or John for not knowing that he was one of the editors. As commended in the Introduction, the subject matter is also considered in *Rights of Light, The Modern Law*.

For our purposes, the most important qualities of an easement are the last two in the list, and we shall therefore spend a little time on them. In a way, the third is the same as the first, but not quite. Perhaps the easiest way to examine the third is by considering rights of way over portions of land we might call Whiteacre and Blackacre. If the same chap owns both, then when he walks from Blackacre onto Whiteacre, he does so *not* because he has a right to do so as the owner of Blackacre, but because he has a right to do so as the owner of

Whiteacre. If someone else owns Whiteacre, however, and yet the owner of Blackacre habitually walks across the former's land – perhaps because it is a useful short-cut – then he may in time acquire a right to do so, even if the owner of Whiteacre wants to stop him. It is quite clear, therefore, that there must be two separate owners (characteristic 3). (That there must be two separate tenements (characteristic 1) seems self-evident.) So there it is – or they are.

There is one interesting side point here. Whereas in the case of most easements a tenant cannot prescribe against his landlord, he can do so for light. Normally, any 'rights' which he enjoys are held through the right of his landlord and as, see above, you have got to have two different people, a tenant cannot have an easement in the right of his landlord over his landlord's other property – except, in the case of light. The fourth characteristic, that the right must be capable of being the subject of a grant, means that the right must be a clearly defined one, which could be put into words and made binding on the servient tenement. This may seem easy – but it is a lot easier to do with positive easements than with negative easements, and a negative easement is what a right to light is. Let's examine that term a little more closely.

A negative easement

A negative easement is not a right for you to do something, but a right to *stop* your neighbour from doing something himself on his own land. It has been argued that this is not capable of forming the subject matter of a grant (and in *Dalton v Angus,* 1881, it was even contended that support was in a similar category).

Fortunately for rights of light consultants it seems now to be established beyond question that a right to light *is* an easement, so we need not enter into recondite legal arguments here.

Easement to a view – or sunlight

John would firmly assert that there was no easement to a view or to sunlight (note that sunlight is not the same as daylight – see Chapter 14). In doing so, he would refer to his father's opinion – a worthy opinion, as his father was arguably the leading practitioner of his day as well – that the incidence of sunlight in this part of the world is far too uncertain for the law to interest itself in the matter. However, John would also draw attention to the increasing use of solar panels and their requirement to make use of every scrap of sunlight that parsimonious Nature can throw at them, such that the intrusion of a substantial obstruction to that sunlight could lead to someone who had spent a small fortune on his solar installation being prepared to risk a still larger fortune on establishing a new right, even though it would be in the more difficult second division of negative easements.

Lance would add to this that he suspects that few would dispute the positive contribution of sunlight to a residential property. The possibility of a change in the law to accommodate sunlight to residential properties in some form in the future cannot therefore be ruled out. It is also to be remembered that on the back of *Allen v Greenwood*, 1978, it is clear that a court of law may at least take account of sunlight in special circumstances – in this particular case, the obstruction of daylight and sunlight to a greenhouse in which tomatoes were being grown – even if not acknowledging an easement to sunlight as such. A few years ago Lance was involved in the defence of sunlight to an industrial greenhouse in which cos lettuces were grown for supermarket outlets. His client had detailed evidence to back up the argument that sunlight was critical to the proper and healthy growth of his lettuces and although sadly, from a learning perspective, the matter was settled in advance of court action, his client had received a bullish legal opinion on the subject.

What does the right consist of?

Having defined easements, we are still not much further on in our consideration of what exactly a right to light is. Once again, though, it might be easier to start by saying what it is not. It is not a right to receive the same light forever, or to have no obstruction of any kind to one's light. Instead, it is a right to be left with 'a residual quantum adequate according to the ordinary notions of mankind'. Or, to put it another way, to be left with 'enough' light.

In *Colls v Home and Colonial Stores,* 1904, Lord Lindley said that a dominant owner was entitled to 'sufficient light according to the ordinary notions of mankind for the comfortable use and enjoyment of his house as a dwelling house', while Lord Davey said that he had a right to enough light 'for the ordinary purposes of inhabitancy or business of the tenement according to the ordinary notions of mankind'.

What, then, are the ordinary notions of mankind? It often seems to be the case that they are, in law, a good deal less than the man on the Clapham omnibus thinks that they are. As this may seem to be a contradiction in terms, it might help to explain a little further. This book devotes a whole chapter to the measurement of light (Chapter 11), so we will only provide a vague outline of the technicalities here.

The 50/50 rule

It was for many years held to be a good working rule that, if a room was left with half its area, at the working plane, lit to a certain minimal standard, then that room, however much light it had lost through neighbouring redevelopment or otherwise, was not actionably injured. That minimum standard was one lumen, the equivalent of the light from a standard candle at one-foot distance. This, the so called 50/50 rule, was upset by the ruling in *Ough v King*, 1967, where a room left adequately lit over *more* than 50% of its area was still deemed actionably injured. However, no other standard was substituted in this case. Since, as Solon said, it is better for the law to be certain than for it to be just, this has led to an unfortunate uncertainty, as no one, not even the most wise, experienced and skilful consultant, can now advise an owner with absolute certainty as to his position.

Nevertheless, the 50/50 rule remains a good general guide in respect of commercial properties at least, and most practitioners use it most of the time. However, in city centres, where expectations – in terms of light at least – are less, a court may well be prepared to award damages in lieu of an injunction even if less than 50% of a room's area were going to remain adequately lit. Dealing with the impact upon residential properties is a little different and Lance would usually advise clients to err on the side of caution and seek to leave an affected room adequately lit over at least 55% of its area wherever possible. The law does not differentiate between commercial and residential buildings as such, but it is Lance's experience that courts tend to be rather more protective of the light to residential properties when considering the question of injunction applications.

The incidence of light at the working plane (838.2mm above floor level, not at floor level itself) is measured by reference to the amount of sky which can be seen from the spot being tested. As will be explained later, this can be related back to the 'one lumen' standard.

Conclusion

We can sum up this chapter by saying that a right to light is an easement; that the right is to have daylight available from the sky; that you are entitled only to adequacy, and not more; and that adequacy is something like half the room sufficiently well lit at approximately table-top level. This long-standing approach is considered further in later chapters, in particular as to whether this is still the correct approach or one that needs updating.

How to acquire a right to light

It might seem strange that we entitle this chapter 'How to acquire a right to light' – and yet that is precisely the situation. You don't just automatically *have* a right to light – you must acquire one.

Of the ways of acquiring a right to light there are principally these five methods: express grant; implied grant; lost modern grant; time immemorial; and the *Prescription Act* 1832; but the most common of these is the *Prescription Act*.

Express grants and reservations

Since it is an essential characteristic of an easement that it should be capable of forming the subject matter of a grant, it must follow that you can acquire a right to light by express grant. An express grant is just what it says: a formal document (or part of one) in which one party specifically grants the other a right to receive light to certain windows. An express reservation is like unto it, and forms part of some other document, usually a contract for sale. A vendor of a site for development, for example, might reserve to himself a right of light to certain windows in a building adjoining the site, thus effectively stopping the purchaser from constructing whatever takes his fancy on his new site. Since, you will doubtless remember from Chapter 1, you cannot have a right of light over your *own* land, those windows would not otherwise have any rights over the land being sold off.

In many ways, express grants (and for grant, read also reservation in this context) are the most difficult to deal with, because they can be expressed in such vague and imprecise terms. We may have complained in Chapter 1 about the uncertainty into which *Ough v King* plunged the 50/50 rule, when dealing with prescriptive rights, but that is a law of the Medes and the Persians compared with the flexible scale of the express grant.

Part of the problem is that there is no set format for this kind of document. Although, of necessity, precise terms and wording will vary from one project to another, this does lead to a multitude of variations on the theme, some better – by which we really mean clearer – than others. What tends to happen is that the solicitor on one side prepares a draft version using his own words, perhaps lifted in part from a previous project, but prior to finalisation it is amended umpteen times while the respective solicitors fight for their preferred form of words. It sometimes ends up as an unsatisfactory hybrid, which, at some stage down the line, creates further dispute and confusion, the need for Counsel's opinion, etc. It is not necessarily reasonable to place all the blame upon the solicitors (although it is surely better than blaming surveyors) but, from a surveyor's perspective, solicitors do provide a rather convenient target!

Express grant provisions can vary enormously and can involve extremes. John was once asked to advise on a deed in which the clause granting a right of light to a certain Livery Hall was so widely drawn that, if you erected a flagstaff which could be seen by a man with his nose pressed hard up against the glass of one of the Hall windows, you would be offending against the grant. This was, as John noted, a disastrous predicament to have let oneself in for. By contrast, however, some express grants do no more than give immediate rights to windows, as if they had acquired them by prescription – which follows later in this chapter.

So beware of express grants, and if you are involved with them, read them very carefully before deciding how much protection they give you, or how much difficulty they are going to cause you in building. This is when it may be well worth taking Counsel's opinion, if the meaning is at all doubtful.

Implied grants

Implied grants are much easier to deal with. They only give rise to the equivalent of prescriptive rights (we're getting closer towards our discussion of them) and they arise in virtually only one set of circumstances. When someone sells off a building with windows in it which rely on light passing over land retained by the vendor, that building gets an implied grant of light to those windows. It would obviously be a derogation from grant, and the purchaser would not get what he had bargained for if, as soon as he had bought his house/office/factory, the vendor erected a solid wall in front of some important windows.

If you are the vendor and you want to be able to build in front of windows in a building you are selling, you have to put an express reservation in the contract (we will have more to say about this later, particularly in relation to the *Newcastle-under-Lyme Squash Club* case). Note that any specific grant, express or implied, is almost certain to give rise to an immediate right. Other methods of acquisition take longer.

Lost modern grant

The 'lost modern grant' is often regarded as a difficult concept to grasp. John was not alone in his wish that it, together with time immemorial (to which we're coming), had been abolished when the *Prescription Act* (to which we are also coming, although you may be beginning to doubt it) was passed. However, it still exists, despite the fact that John only knew of it ever having been pleaded in one case. Although Lance often feels the need to mention it in his reports, he also has not yet had it pleaded in a single case with which he has been involved. The idea is that if you are enjoying a right over someone else's property, and they cannot prove that it is by permission which they can withdraw, then obviously you must have a grant somewhere entitling you to that right. The only trouble is, you can't put your hand on it just at the moment. Nevertheless, the fact that you must have had one at some time is so obvious that it is deemed to exist. It has just been 'lost'. And if you think that's nonsense, then you're in good company – but who are we to make judgments on the law?

Let's be clear about this: it is entirely a fictitious legal assumption. Everyone knows there wasn't a grant, and that you haven't just mislaid it. In one important leading case, *Dalton v Angus*, 1881, it was agreed on all sides that no grant in fact existed, yet it was presumed to do so for the purposes of the case. The most important point about the lost grant is that it may allow you several years in which to bring an action, whereas prescription (to which, yes, we are still coming) only allows one year. That is certainly the reason for its use in the case mentioned above. In the case of a claim pursued under the *Prescription Act*, if the affected party (the dominant tenement) fails to take substantive action in defence of its light within a year, it will probably be deemed to have acquiesced and its right of action will be lost. A matter pursued under the doctrine of the lost modern grant, however, brings into effect the Statute of Limitations and thus there could be a six-year period to play with.

The other use of the lost modern grant is in claiming against the Crown, because it used to be accepted – and this may still be correct, but not necessarily so and we will come onto that shortly – that one could not acquire an easement of light against the Crown under section 3 of the *Prescription Act*, because Crown land was exempt. That being so, lost modern grant provides a possible alternative method of claiming rights against the Crown.

The term of enjoyment needed in order to acquire a right under the lost modern grant is not laid down anywhere (which is extremely helpful!). It is therefore perhaps reasonable to conclude that it must be longer than under the *Prescription Act* and shorter than time immemorial (see below); John guessed at about 30 years as a minimum, but this really was mere conjecture on his part, and we are thus still left to wonder. By this point you might be beginning to agree with Lance and John in terms of their love-hate relationship with this doctrine.

In recent times, a further twist has arisen in respect of this particular tale with reference to the *Human Rights*

Act 1998. There is now increasing uncertainty as to the validity of the Crown immunity argument. This point is explored in a little more detail in Chapter 16.

Time immemorial

John never had a time immemorial case and admitted to being reasonably desperate for one, to complete his set. While Lance has never felt quite the same yearning himself, he agrees that it would certainly be interesting. The reason for the lack of cases is simply because there are so few opportunities for one to arise. In brief, 'time immemorial' refers to circumstances in which, if you can show that you have enjoyed a right since 'the time whereof the memory of man runneth not to the contrary', then that, like all these other methods of acquisition, establishes your right. Unfortunately, according to the law, that time is 1189, so it's a bit hard to prove.

John could offer no official explanation as to why 1189 is considered the date of legal memory, and therefore simply provided the conjecture below. Once upon a time, the date of legal memory used to be changed regularly. Every time a new king came to the throne (or perhaps on some other important occasion), the lawyers sat down and said something like: there's no man living now who can remember the Norman Conquest, so that's the date where we'll fix time immemorial. Then they fixed another date, and so on and so on until they came to 1189, which they probably fixed in 1275 or thereabouts. But another important event, or coronation, came along very soon afterwards, and they didn't bother to change the date; and next time they forgot; and next time it was so well-established that they didn't like to change it. So there it remains to this day. The book by Stephen Bickford Smith and Andrew Francis confirms that the date was fixed by the Statute of Westminster in 1275 and remains fixed.

Prescription

And finally, comes the *Prescription Act* 1832 (and we've saved the best until last – or certainly, the most common means of acquiring a right to light in law until last). It having been realised that the time immemorial method and the lost modern grant were a bit unwieldy – and perhaps unreliable – the long title of this Act announced that it was 'an Act for shortening the Time of Prescription in certain cases'. It did not, however, abolish other methods of acquiring rights. In brief, this Act allows you to acquire a right by 'prescription', which means that if you enjoy a right for a certain period (in this case, 20 years) without interruption, it becomes, in effect, an established legal right.

Section 3 of the *Prescription Act* deals specifically with rights of light, and differs in several important respects from the other sections. A comparative study is not necessary for our purposes here, but as mentioned earlier, it does not mention and thus arguably not bind, any royal hereditaments – the Crown. The period of prescription is set at 20 years 'next before some suit or action' (this means some legal action, not just 'doing something'). The 20 years' enjoyment must be 'without interruption', and interruption is stated in section 4 to require a period of one year. As you cannot have a year's interruption within a 20-year period after 19 years and one day have passed, it follows that effectively a right is acquired after the shorter period. You cannot, however, mount a legal action to uphold your right until the full 20 years is up: more of that later.

Rights of Light Act

Finally, in this chapter, a word about the *Rights of Light Act* 1959. This did not really have much to do with rights of light, but apart from its more important innovations, which are dealt with in a later chapter, it had an ephemeral effect which has occasionally given rise to some confusion. Because it was extremely difficult during the Second World War years to stop anyone acquiring a right to light, the period of prescription was extended under this Act, for a limited time, to 27 years. This relaxation has already lapsed, but it has been known for people to think that it was a permanent alteration and still effective. It isn't: we are back to 20 years prescription.

How to hold on to it

'It' refers to the right to light which you have so painstakingly acquired in the last chapter, of course.

By far the best way of preserving light to your windows is to own all the land around your building, at least for a time, and then only to sell off that land with a very clearly expressed reservation (see Chapter 2), preserving as extensive a right as you wish. However, this counsel of near perfection is hardly available to any of us except the great estate owners, and so we shall have to consider other methods.

The first thing to tell you, in your effort to hold onto your rights, is the need for eternal vigilance – and prompt action when required. You may have a prescriptive claim to light, but it needs only one year's interruption of your right to defeat your claim. It is all too easy to allow an argument about a possible injury to drag on until one year has passed; at which point, theoretically at least, your light has been legally interrupted and your prescriptive right has been lost. (In fact, where two parties are in active negotiation – particularly if it is simply a matter of agreeing a suitable compensation sum – the developing party does not usually try to invoke this provision simply because matters have not been settled within the one-year period. As John pointed out, that is particularly true where two large property owners are in negotiation, because to stand on ceremony in one case might rebound upon them in another.) It has been suggested to Lance that in order to avoid this problem, the injured party has to have taken 'substantive action'. Issuing legal proceedings is undoubtedly the safest approach, but clear protest and expression of dissent, preferably in writing, might suffice.

The interruption has to be with notice, and must be acquiesced in by the dominant owner. The subject of notice is rather tricky, and there are no immediately obvious cases in which it has been expressly discussed, but it would seem that it is not enough surreptitiously to obscure some light, and then claim that you or your neighbour has suffered interruption. On the other hand, it does seem that you are not obliged to write to your neighbour and tell him.

Acquiescence does have a useful leading case to explain it. In *Dance v Triplow*, 1992, the Court of Appeal decided that two and a half years' silence on the part of either the claimant or his solicitor, even when objections had previously been voiced, would lead a reasonable man to assume that his neighbour had now accepted the situation. The Court distinguished the case from that of *Davies v Du Paver*, 1953, where the claim form was issued 13 months after the last previous objection. As one has to acquiesce for a year, acquiescence in the latter case would have had to begin only a month after a forceful protest – which was unlikely.

As we note above, between two large property owners, precise time limits are unlikely to be insisted upon, if serious negotiations have been taking place, as next week/month/year the boot may be on the other foot. There is no doubt, however, that there are a number of bully boys around in the development world who would quite happily stand on the letter of the law if the little man next door should miss a trick. So, if negotiations should stall, do not allow too much time to pass before you issue your claim form.

The worst case scenario is losing one's right of action because of delay, but acting promptly can also make the difference between one's ability to obtain an injunction and having to settle for damages. Even if an injury potentially warranted an injunction, a court would be less likely to grant one if it decided that the injured party had been dilatory, such that an injunction would no longer be an equitable remedy. Lance has known potential claimants deliberately delay in the hope of pouncing at a later and more critical stage, but that is a dangerous tactic and could easily backfire. If you really want to protect your light, act as quickly as possible.

So, to sum up: if you are sure that your light is injured – usually, after taking advice from a specialist consultant – you must get a legal action under way within one year of the injury occurring. The preliminary steps do not cost a great deal of money; they should ensure that your adversary knows that you mean business; and, provided that the advice you receive is sound, you should recover costs – at least in part – in due course. It is good sense to take action as soon as possible.

It seems almost unnecessary to say so, except that a few cases have proved otherwise, but don't lightly enter into agreements with others which may give them the right to injure your light at a later date. Sometimes you may be seeking a concession from them: perhaps you are adding to your building in such a way that you are affecting their light and so, as well as paying compensation, you are being asked to enter into a deed which allows your opponents to rebuild in the future without so much as a by-your-leave. Your present proposals may put you in such a position that they could enjoin you if they so choose (and their chances of doing so are dealt with later) so that you either have to agree with their proposed deed or else alter your building. You may prefer to give in – but if you don't have to, don't.

As a kind of early warning system, be alert to planning proposals. If you can persuade the planners to refuse permission for a proposed building which would injure your light, it comes much cheaper than waiting until the servient owner has got permission and then bringing an action at law. As a matter of tactics, however, don't stress your intention to sue – if necessary – when talking or writing to the planners. That might just, if they were hesitating, persuade them to grant permission, telling themselves that you will, in any event, be protected from ill effects, if any, by your legal rights. Keep more to the unneighbourliness of your opponents' proposals, by all means stressing the effect upon your daylight, but also bringing in matters with which planners are concerned (though the law is not), such as sunshine, view, and general ambience.

It has taken at least 20 years for you to acquire your right to light. Don't throw it away by being slack in its defence.

A brief note on consultants and experts

It might be appropriate at this point to say a word about rights of light consultants. Good ones are rather thin on the ground, and yet it is important to take advice from surveyors with experience and detailed knowledge of the subject. Lance used to think that the RICS should keep a list – a very limited one – of true experts in the field, but recognises that in reality there would be almost insurmountable difficulties in compiling and revising it – because who would decide who should be on it? The lay client is therefore in some difficulty. However, whenever Lance finds himself unable to deal with a matter – not enough time, a conflict of interests, or whatever – he is always willing to pass on the names of other suitable consultants, irrespective of whether he is dealing with a longstanding client or a potential new one – and believes that the other few experts with sufficient experience in the field would behave in a similar fashion. For readers suitably intrigued, he is therefore sure he could give a few names over the telephone without causing offence.

For those of you who may fancy yourselves as rights of light consultants, or are thinking of setting up your plate, the authors have some further advice (with more contained in Chapter 15). John recounted the fact that when his father, Bryan Anstey, gave him a personally inscribed copy of his book, *The Right To Light* (Estates Gazette), he wrote inside the cover: 'I sincerely hope that study of this book will not lead anyone to think himself an expert'. Recognising the truth in that, John likewise emphasised that reading the first three editions of this book would not turn anyone into an expert, but might leave them better informed than when they opened the front cover. Lance would expand upon John's point by reiterating the danger arising out of surveyors taking on rights of light instructions when they are not sufficiently experienced and qualified to do so. He often hears fellow surveyors – sometimes friends as well as professional colleagues – explaining that they only deal with 'simple' rights of light matters and pass things on to experts when the need arises. The trouble is, that without sufficient experience, the surveyor will struggle to identify what truly is a simple issue – and by the time they find out, it may be too late. It is sadly the case that many surveyors take on rights of light instructions when the work relates to an established client, because they are fearful of admitting to limitations in their knowledge and have an aversion to recommending the name of others more suitable for the task. Not only is that a recipe for disaster, but it should be remembered that most rights of light specialists do not do any other form of work and are thus not a professional threat to their colleagues anyway. (Lance would stress that he does not make this point in the hope of obtaining further instructions, being already obliged to turn away a number of the instructions offered to him, but simply to make the point that surveyors do themselves, and those seeking their help, a disservice by taking on instructions beyond the limits of their particular abilities.)

How to defeat acquisition

Some people want to acquire a right to light – others want to defeat that acquisition. It's that basic dichotomy that keeps the wheels of rights to light firms turning.

There are basically two ways to defeat acquisition: the theoretical and the physical. The exciting thing about one of the theoretical ways is that it is theoretically physical. That remark is intended to intrigue you, and to keep up the suspense, as we shall not deal with that aspect until the end of the chapter. As the chapters are all fairly short, at least you know that the suspense won't be intolerable.

Avoiding conceding a right

Perhaps we should say at the outset, although this really is blindingly obvious, that one way of stopping someone from acquiring any right is not to grant it to them. Do not, unless it is absolutely forced upon you in circumstances which make it impossible for you to refuse, concede a right to any windows which already exist or are being opened. If you do, they could well come back to haunt you (that may be a little graphic, but I'm sure you know what we mean).

Precario

Any easement must be acquired *nec vi, nec clam, nec precario*: not by force, nor secretly, nor precariously. The last word in the translation there is intended to catch the flavour of *precario*, which in fact comes from *preces*, Latin for prayers, and came to mean 'upon request', or 'dependent upon the will of others', before it reached the definition we understand. It certainly means that you mustn't be likely to lose the easement at a moment's notice.

The first two prohibitions are not really likely to apply to rights of light: they are more important in rights of way or profits à prendre. If you knock a man down every time he tries to tell you that you have no right to walk across his back garden to get to the bus stop, you cannot claim that you have always walked that way by right. Similarly, if you only sneak into the next-door market garden to help yourself to cauliflowers under cover of darkness, you can hardly assert your right to continue doing so in the daylight.

Precario often applies to windows, however. Deed after deed records that 'the windows coloured blue on the elevation lettered X-Y on the land coloured pink adjoining the land coloured green and hatched black on the plan lettered B enjoy their light over the aforesaid land coloured green by permission of the adjoining owners', or words to that effect. Whenever new windows appear, overlooking your land, you should therefore endeavour to persuade the owners of them to enter into some such deed or licence.

If you can so carry your point, you may be asked to limit your own freedom to build for the future. You may feel

23

able to agree to such a restriction, in which case you should try to be sure, first, that you stipulate that any limits to projected building will still enable you to erect a building which is big enough for anything you may want to do, and, secondly, that the limiting clause is a permissive one, not restrictive. This is such a complicated issue that it demands a – short – chapter of its own (Chapter 6).

A neighbourly letter

It is not, in the authors' opinion, necessary to have a formal legal deed in order to prove that windows have *no* right to light, although large corporations may well want to have one. A letter from your next-door neighbour acknowledging that he has no right to light should be quite sufficient, and you may well be able to extract one from him by threatening more physical measures if he does not comply. By which the authors do not mean offering to knock him down (although it might make the chapter more entertaining if they did). For commentary on physical measures, see below.

Reservation in a deed of sale

If you are disposing of a property with windows, or land on which such a property might be built, while retaining other land (or even thinking of acquiring other land) over which the aforesaid windows look or may look, do not forget to put a reservation in the deed of sale which allows you to build or to permit building regardless of its effect upon the light of these windows – or any other which may appear in that vicinity. You may never need the right, but it's silly to miss the opportunity of securing it, and it may well make your retained property more saleable should you later come to dispose of it as well.

And the physical ways

So much for most of the theoretical ways. The physical ways are obvious. Block 'em up (the windows, that is). Tempting as it is to leave this paragraph here, we should perhaps expand a little. The best way of stopping any window acquiring a right to light is by stopping it from getting any light. No light, no right. And while you can't really physically go round blocking up your neighbour's windows, you *can* physically stop them getting light in other ways. For example, if you are in a position to construct a building before any windows looking at it have acquired any rights, stand not upon the order of your building, but build at once, and don't dilly-dally on the way to their acquisition. A really solid brick wall in the way of the windows is definitely the preferable solution, but a dense screen of evergreen foliage might be equally effective (see Chapter 7 on trees too). You can also erect a fence, or put up a hoarding, and you can even construct curious devices to block one, new, window only, in a wall full of rightful apertures.

The theoretically physical

The difficulty about these physical obstructions, quite apart from the plant life, is that they may well require planning permission – which brings us to the theoretically physical. Before Town and Country Planning became all the rage after the Second World War, the accepted way of stopping a window from acquiring a right was, as noted in the paragraph above, to erect a hoarding in front of it. Indeed, the 13th edition of *Gale*, published in the very year in which these matters changed, says: 'The conventional method of interrupting the access of light, in order to prevent the acquisition of an easement, is by the erection of a screen or hoarding near the boundary of the prospectively servient property'. That's exactly what we say above, only put more learnedly, and it means putting up some opaque object near the edge of your land, confronting the new windows.

Unfortunately, since it became impossible to put up a fence more than two metres high without planning permission, and as very few fences of that height would be any use in interrupting light (though, as a matter of fact, one would have obliterated Mr Metaxides' light, referred to in the chapter on trees – see Chapter 7), it seemed as if dominant owners were going to find it a lot easier in future to attain their dominance. A way had to be found to redress the balance and, in 1959, as the second and still very effective part of the *Rights of Light Act*, a device was brought into being which put the servient owner back into much the same position that he had previously occupied. The only difference was that, instead of paying a builder to erect a hoarding, he now had to pay a surveyor, perhaps (good), and a lawyer (perhaps not so good) to create something altogether different. Some surveyors have now taken to preparing and issuing the necessary forms themselves, but Lance prefers to provide background advice and prepare any necessary drawings, leaving his client's lawyers to ensure that all the proper paperwork is in place.

Notional obstruction

What is this magical device? It is best known as a 'Notional Obstruction' – although the authors have encountered people dealing with such matters who did not know it by that title (let us hope that they buy this book). It is simply a paper substitute for a physical obstruction.

The procedure is as follows: if windows are about to
acquire a right against you, you prepare a plan showing
the windows and your boundary, and you nominate the
size of notional screen you intend to erect (theoretically)
along this boundary, which can be of unlimited height.
You prepare a Notice of Notional Obstruction and you
take it, with the plan, to the Lands Tribunal. They give
directions on how it is to be publicised to the affected,
would-be dominant owners, and when those directions
have been followed, the Notice is entered on the local
Registry of Land Charges, where it stays for a year. Thus,
since one year's interruption is sufficient to defeat a
prescriptive right, no such right is obtained by any
immature windows, and they must start to prescribe all
over again. If you are scared that the windows are just on
the point of attaining their majority, you can ask for
immediate registration as a matter of urgency. The Lands
Tribunal will, if satisfied as to the necessity, grant
registration for four months, which will then be extended
to the full 12 when proof of the subsequent publicity to
the affected properties is produced. If you do not comply
with the directions – and if, perchance, the dominant
owner proves that he has already established his right –
then the registration will lapse after four months and no
interruption will have taken place.

Where the windows in the relevant neighbouring property
have not yet reached maturity, in the vast majority of
cases it is folly to specify an obstruction of anything but
unlimited height. However, there are a couple of
variations on that theme that need to be considered. The
first is where the neighbouring property has established
rights in law by prescription, but the original buildings
on the development site have been demolished such that
in the fullness of time – 20 years – the neighbouring

property will acquire increased rights, in the cleared site condition. In that instance, the Light Obstruction Notice may take the form of a notional obstruction depicting the height and massing of the previously demolished buildings, rather than a simple, opaque structure of unlimited height. The second is where the neighbouring building has a mixture of immature and well-established windows. In that instance it may be necessary to specify some curiously shaped and detailed screen. (There may well also be occasions when you are unable to do anything about the windows at all.) The problem you face is that the notional obstruction – whatever shape or form it takes – must not be such that it would cause an actionable loss of light to any of the established windows. Therefore, for example, if a building has established windows along the whole of its ground floor, it is difficult to envisage any form of obstruction that would work against the windows on the floors above, yet not impinge upon the ground floor openings. In such a case – perhaps an extreme example, but far from impossible – the existence of the established ground-floor openings could indirectly serve to protect all of the immature windows on the floors above as well.

In general one should avoid serving Light Obstruction Notices on established windows, as the notice will then be too easy to defeat and your actions will have alerted the neighbour to the fact that you think you have a rights of light problem. However, increasingly, solicitors advise their clients to issue Light Obstruction Notices without necessarily carrying out detailed research on the relevant windows and without a great deal of care as to whether the windows have established rights or not. This must simply be because there are occasions where affected neighbours fail to respond and deal with Light

Obstruction Notices, such that in the fullness of time they lose their rights. Perhaps there is therefore some merit in this approach, but the author still has reservations.

Two problems with notional obstructions

There are two main problems which arise from notional obstructions. The authors do not have a really satisfactory answer to either, but at least you have been warned of their existence.

There is a theoretical answer to the first problem, but it does not always seem to work in practice. When a notice has been on the local register for a year, it has done its work, and the notionally obstructed windows may then begin to prescribe all over again. If, however, someone searches the register, a short while later, what do they find? If they find nothing, they may conclude that the windows have a right to light. They should find evidence that a notice has been registered and that, therefore, until 19 years have passed since its year of registration ended, no rights will be established. A search during the notice's actual currency would surely reveal its presence, but the authors have known a number of instances where searches during the following years have not shown up its former but still effective existence. If you have any reason to suspect that a notice may at some time have been registered – or perhaps even if you haven't – you should specifically enquire of the council whether one was on the register at any time in the preceding 19 years.

The second problem is a technical legal one, and no doubt a lawyer or two will write to tell Lance the answer (he can only say that he knows of no case in which the issue has yet been tested). A notice of notional obstruction will defeat a prescriptive right, because one year's interruption is enacted so to do in the 1832 Act: but what effect will it have on an express or a lost modern grant? Consider. If you claim a right under the *Prescription Act*, one year's interruption defeats it. Therefore, you have only one year in which to bring an action to defend the right. The same is true of the effect of a notice of notional obstruction. You have a year from its registration in which to bring an action, after which the right is lost irrespective of whether it is the permanent or emergency variety. On the other hand, if you claim a right under an express grant, or a lost modern grant, one year's interruption is not enough to defeat it. Therefore, you have several years in which to bring an action to defend the right. The same cannot be true, surely, of the effect of a notice of notional obstruction, particularly as that effect will cease when the year of its registration comes to an end. In that case, the failure of the 1832 Act to abolish other forms of prescription, coupled with the 1959 Act's intended simplification of obstruction, will have resulted in another little anomaly.

How to deal with someone else's right

There are, in effect, four different ways of dealing with other peoples' rights to light when involved in development: ensure your building is designed to avoid causing an actionable infringement; build anyway, and chance it; make a direct approach to the neighbours offering to pay compensation; or put the neighbours on notice of your intention without specifically referring to rights of light, in the hope that their case will be prejudiced if they fail to react and object. There may be subtle variations on these themes, but they are, fundamentally, the options available to the developing party.

The first option does not seem to find much favour, but John achieved a certain notoriety from one such case. In this particular proposed redevelopment, there were a number of really tricky situations. So, working together, the architects and John trimmed the building to the state where, at all sensitive points, it was wholly within the existing profile. A great meeting of the professional team was summoned by the clients and everyone assembled in a massive hall: about 50 people, including clients, architects, quantity surveyors, engineers, services engineers, Old Uncle Tom Cobleigh and all. Tea and biscuits were served, and the proceedings began. Each element in turn was asked to report on the state of the game from his point of view, which each did, at some length. When John's turn came, he stood up and said (and this is his speech in its entirety): 'Everything we propose to do is either covered by deeds or, being within the existing building's outline, has no effect on the neighbours'. And he sat down again. 'Isn't there anything else you'd like to say, Mr Anstey?' asked the head client. 'Yes', John replied, 'I've been trying to get another biscuit for ten minutes'. They didn't ask him to any more meetings.

We'll return to that option again a little later on. For now, we'll concentrate on the more frequently used ones.

Build and chance it

There is no duty at law to go and negotiate with anyone who may have a right to light: you are not committing a criminal act by building even in such a way as drastically to reduce the light to their most important windows. The 'build and chance it' option – obtaining planning permission if you need it and commencing on site without reference to your neighbours – is therefore worthy of consideration, but obviously involves a degree of risk, and a significant risk if the impact is clearly actionable rather than borderline. Lance is surprised by how many developers adopt this bullish approach and get away with it, sometimes not even paying a penny of compensation when they were exposed to the risk of injunction, but he would reiterate that you could be taking an awful risk. While this is probably a risk worth taking in certain cases, such an unneighbourly approach is likely to be frowned upon by a court if you are unfortunate and the neighbour reacts and litigation ensues. Your building works might then be injuncted (although technically, the word is 'enjoined'), with disastrous consequences. There are times where the consultant needs to be bold and advise his client that this route may be the best ploy, but ensure that the client fully understands the risks involved, otherwise a claim form served on you is likely to follow hard on the heels of the claim form served on your client.

We go into much more detail about injunctions and their possible cost to the dominant owner in the chapter on remedies (Chapter 10), and utter there a warning about overstepping the line between damages and an injunction. In this chapter, we are really only looking at things from a developer's point of view, be he a multi-million-pound property company or the householder building a bedroom over the garage.

From the developer's point of view, an injunction is a disaster. True, you may recover damages yourself if the application for an interlocutory one was ill-founded (see again Chapter 10 on remedies), but you're bound to be out of pocket anyway, not to mention the nuisance and disturbance of it all. However, let us assume that the adjoining dominant owner was not so silly as to rush off to court without being advised that he had a good case, and that the injunction is not only sought but obtained. What does the developer do then? Apart from having to amend his building, seek a revised planning consent and so on, he probably looks around for someone to blame; possibly the architect, but more likely the rights of light consultant if he advised him to proceed.

An injunction stops the developer dead in his tracks. The wording of it will be to the effect that you cannot build so as to injure the light of your neighbour, and that may mean that you will be confined to the outline of the previous building on your site. Your foundations may be all wrong for such a building, and the planning of your accommodation may be completely disrupted because you can no longer put the core where you intended. Your programme will run late, you may have to renegotiate a letting, you'll be out of pocket on costs and you won't have the amount of space to let (or use) that you thought you would have. As we said above: a disaster.

Returning to the first option

Assuming you are the type of person (or organisation) whose vocabulary does not include 'build and chance it', there are three more alternatives to consider, the safest of which of course is to eliminate all risk by carefully designing your building to avoid any actionable impact upon a neighbour's light. Anstey Horne & Co is regularly employed to advise – often based upon detailed studies using specialist computer software – as to what the 'safe' massing on a site would be, and this is therefore a valid consideration. However, on some sites it would prevent you building much, if at all, beyond the confines of your existing building envelope. More often than not, what the developer is actually trying to establish is how much more he might be able to get away with. What developers really want is to combine maximum development value with a risk-free solution, but alas (and this is pretty obvious really), those two aspirations rarely go hand in hand.

Compensating the neighbours

This is the third option mentioned above. If you decide to approach your neighbour with a view to bringing the matter out into the open, you will have to handle things with great tact and delicacy. It's not really the best tactic to say, 'I'm going to ruin your light, and you could get an injunction to stop me, so how much does it need to buy you off?'. That is rather asking to be taken advantage of. It's equally unwise to assume brashly that you can get away with it, and try to pooh-pooh the other side's rights. That is likely to put their backs up instead, with much the same end-result. The best approach is an open and friendly one, but with a degree of confidence, for example, 'You know that I'm about to build next door. Here are my plans. I think that your light may be injured a little, and of course I'm perfectly ready to pay the proper sum in compensation. If you would like to instruct a consultant to agree the money with mine, I'd be pleased to pay his fees'. There's no guarantee that the dominant owners – or their consultant – may not reply 'I'll see you in court' or words to that effect, but at least you have given yourself a chance.

Remember that in all these cases, the pace of discussions will be dictated by the injured party – the dominant owner. There are some clients who will demand that you have all the rights of light tied up before the contractor starts on site. You can tell them to find another consultant – or you can explain gently to them that the only way of doing that is with a series of blank cheques, and co-operative opponents. If the dominant owner doesn't want to rush, the only thing that is likely to change his mind is a really substantial offer, well over the odds, with a time limit attached for his acceptance of the bribe.

If you want to buy someone out of their rights (which, the courts have stated time and time again, you must not think you are entitled to do so if they are unwilling) you have got to go about it in a conciliatory way, and at their speed. Any urging them along must be done delicately and politely, if you do not wish either to bring the negotiations to an abrupt halt or else to put up the costs to your client by a large 'impatience' factor.

A neighbourly notice

A variation on the direct approach – the fourth of our tactical options – is to proceed down the route of what Lance would generally refer to as a 'neighbourly letter of introduction'. The idea is that one writes to the affected neighbour to introduce the scheme, providing a representative set of plans and notification of your intended programme, inviting any comment or queries the neighbour might have. One does not openly admit to a rights of light infringement or offer to pay compensation – indeed some developers go weak at the knees at the thought of such an admission – but if the neighbour fails to respond and object, he may well have prejudiced his ability to obtain an injunction if he reacts and seeks to cause trouble at a later and more critical stage. It can therefore be a useful tactic, but does not of course provide the certainty arising out of an amended, safe building profile or advance agreement to pay compensation.

The timing of this kind of letter is important and one has to give careful consideration to whether it should be issued pre or post planning in case it stirs up unwanted planning objections, but the overriding concern must be to ensure that the notice is issued at an early stage (early enough for the parties receiving it to have a reasonable period of time to consider the position and respond before the relevant works commence). If the recipient is dilatory in response that could well be prejudicial to their case, but that is not an argument one could successfully pursue in front of a judge if the letter had only been issued a very short while before commencement of the works. In those circumstances, the court would be perfectly at liberty to take the view that the developer had only himself to blame for the fact that objections had appeared at a late and critical stage.

Ancient lights

A quick word here about 'ancient lights', which often comes up in these situations. Many people think that a sign bearing the words 'Ancient Lights' has some secret and wonderful powers, and that unless you have such a sign, your windows will never acquire their right to light in its full potency. In fact, the sign means nothing, and has virtually no value at all, except that it proclaims to the world that the holder believes he has a right to light, and is likely to be strong in its defence. If you see such a sign on someone's windows which you are going to affect, you should watch out. You should almost certainly make a direct approach, because you would not look convincing if you tried to tell the court that you didn't realise that your neighbour had any right to light.

6 Permissive and restrictive deeds

Neither Lance nor John have ever been shy of providing an opinion on those matters which overlap with the expertise of the legal profession – and deeds is one of those matters. Rights of light consultants are regularly confronted with deeds for interpretation and application to a particular site and deal with these on the basis that although they have no legal training, they have dealt with hundreds of similar documents in conjunction with solicitors or barristers on other projects. Indeed, it is not unrealistic to say that experienced rights of light consultants are probably more familiar with the niceties of this kind of documentation than the majority of practising solicitors.

However – and this is an important word of warning for would-be rights of light surveyors – do not underestimate the skills of the legal profession (particularly specialist barristers) when it comes to the fine interpretation of legal documents, and if you do offer an opinion to a client, make it clear that they must seek the advice of their legal team as well. Not only is that probably sound advice with regard to the question of professional indemnity (PI) insurance, but it is also only right and proper that the client be clear as to the limitations of your expertise. This is perhaps emphasised by what follows below, which should serve to confirm the potentially vital importance of deeds and what they really mean in the context of light.

There is a great deal of confusion as to what constitutes a restrictive deed and what is a permissive one. There are some documents which partake of both natures (we get on to those below), and some which are so open-ended that you wonder why anyone ever bothered to pay solicitors to draw them up. This last kind can be a snare and a delusion to poor innocents, who fancy that they must have some tremendous impact upon future development on one or the other – or both – sides. In reality, this last kind are no more important than a 'release', a very simple document employed in straightforward cases by rights of light consultants, to conclude matters without the need of legal assistance. Lance would add that most rights of light settlements are now concluded with a formal Deed of Release (usually prepared by solicitors) rather than the very simple form referred to below.

A typical release runs thus:

Address   Head Office

or House of

the dominant owner

FORM OF RELEASE

RIGHTS OF LIGHT

Re: The Injured Building and the Proposed One

In consideration of the sum of (so many pounds) the receipt of which is hereby acknowledged, and the

39

payment of fees in the sum of (generally rather less money) direct to (the dominant owner's surveyors and solicitors) we consent to the erection by (the developers) of a building in accordance with the attached drawings nos. (124–125) and undertake for ourselves and on behalf of anyone claiming interest through or under us to raise no objection to such building on account of any interference with light.

For and on behalf of: The dominant owner

Signed: The Boss

Date: Whenever

Restrictive deeds

The most important kind of deed, and one which needs careful keeping and consideration, is the restrictive kind. This says something like: 'The building owner may build according to the attached plans, but no variation from those in any building or rebuilding is to be permitted without the consent of the adjoining owner'. Actually, to tell the truth, it probably says nothing like that at all, because it is all tricked out with legal phraseology, but that is what it means to say, when all superfluity is stripped away. However it is worded, you must carefully scan each deed to see if that is the meaning that lurks within, because to ignore such a prohibition is to court disaster.

The virtually certain remedy (see Chapter 10) for breach of a specific prohibition on building is an injunction. Clients of John's went to Counsel once about a deed which permitted them to build up to 50 feet high all along a certain frontage. They proposed to build 40 feet high for 90% of the length, and 55 feet high for the remainder. The net result would be that the owner with the benefit of the agreement would be better off than if the full freedom of the clause were adopted, yet counsel advised that they were at serious risk if they built those extra five feet without seeking their neighbour's consent.

Escaping from a prohibitive deed can be very costly, even if relaxation is sought before ever work starts. Other than in exceptional circumstances, the neighbour has the developer over a barrel and is in a position, potentially, to demand a king's ransom. Both John and Lance have been involved in cases where compliance with the restrictive terms of a deed would have decimated the development potential of the site and led to literally millions of pounds being paid over to buy off the neighbours. It may, of course, be worthwhile from a developer's point of view to pay over a large sum if he gains enough in return, but it does emphasise the need to examine all deeds minutely, and to look very carefully for any potentially restrictive terminology. As John put it, you must find such words if they exist and explain their input fully to your client. Bearing in mind the potential ramifications arising out of restrictive covenants, you will understand why Lance stresses the need to obtain specialist legal advice on some occasions as well.

Permissive deeds

While permissive deeds are less onerous from a developer's point of view, they are often more complicated to interpret. If that seems paradoxical, it is because while it is usually fairly easy to understand what is prohibited, it can be very difficult to understand what is permitted, or indeed whether the permission is wholehearted or modified. Very often, the permission granted to the side which was not building when the deed was drawn up can be very simple. As part of the price extracted for allowing the first developers to build at all, the erstwhile dominant owner has insisted upon a clause allowing him in future to build anything for which he can get planning permission. On one or two remarkable occasions, wily lawyers have even succeeded in persuading the dominant owners to allow the developers that freedom while restricting their own ability to build in the future. John – and many others – have wondered what the dominant owners' own lawyers were thinking of to let them sign such a document, but not every consideration which goes into an agreement appears on the face of the document.

A permissive arrangement is much less troublesome for a developer, because although the permission may be limited to a certain height and profile, the Deed does not expressly prohibit him from building higher – he may be able to, but normal common law principles would apply where one is impacting upon a neighbour's light, and the tactical options – build and chance it, etc. – apply as set out in Chapter 5. Unfortunately, the difference between a restrictive and permissive arrangement can be very subtle; Lance has seen many deeds where the terminology has flitted between a restrictive and permissive form. Other than blaming the solicitor who drafted the rogue document – and that's not much good if it is a deed drawn up in the 1890s – what else can one do to deal with this dilemma? The developer can of course call his neighbour's bluff and confidently state that the terms are permissive and that he is proceeding with his scheme, but that can be very dangerous indeed.

Prohibitive or permissive?

An example of this problem comes with what we can characterise as the 'but no other' class of deed. Many documents contain a clause which permits a development up to certain dimensions, but no further; or it may allow a building in accordance with the attached plans, but no other. It is far from clear whether the plain and ordinary meaning of those short clauses is prohibitive or permissive. When they are interlarded with legal verbiage it becomes even harder to be sure which meaning should attach to them. It is hard enough even to explain the ambiguity, but we will try.

The first view of the meaning of many such clauses is that their effect is: only the nominated building is permitted; any other building or any variation is prohibited. The second view is that it means: the extent of the permission granted by this deed is stated above, and it doesn't extend any further; if you go beyond these limits you will be subject to the ordinary constraints of rights of light law.

John complained that the trouble was that people (by which he fully admitted to meaning solicitors) will insist on writing their own versions of these clauses, instead of following a really reliable model. He had a point, but from a personal, surveying perspective, Lance would not normally be as bold as John used to be in suggesting that he provide suitable wording himself. The drafting of deeds is specialist in itself and a job for solicitors in the first instance, although most solicitors do recognise the benefit of having a rights of light consultant working with them. It is Lance's opinion that where solicitors run into difficulty is when they try to cover every possible eventuality and permutation. Although this is fine in principle, it can lead to an overcomplicated document that may end up going around in circles and – this is where it happens – producing both restrictive and permissive elements. Because getting the drafting right is so important, and the majority of solicitors would happily admit to not being specialists in the subject of rights of light, Lance would argue that there is some merit in seeking Counsel's opinion on the appropriateness of a deed before it is finalised. After all, everyone seems happy to seek the opinion of Counsel when years later they cannot work out what the deed really says, so there seems to be some sense in being proactive rather than reactive in these instances.

Moving back to John, we can relate the history of the potentially most expensive clause of this kind which ever came his way. He always felt that it would have been no exaggeration to say that millions of pounds rode upon the precise interpretation. A deed was sent to John by solicitors, together with Counsel's opinion that it was a restrictive one. John read both deed and opinion carefully, and responded that, with all due respect to Counsel, whom he knew well to be of high repute in the field, he thought it permissive. His 'opinion' was sent to Counsel, who replied that, with all due respect to John, he adhered to his original view. As so much hung upon the issue, John's clients went to an eminent QC to decide the matter. His opening words were to become one of John's favourite quotations: 'I do not say that there is not a great deal of money to be made out of arguing this point'. He went on to say that if he was forced to side with one or the other, he would reluctantly disagree with his learned friend and agree with Mr Anstey.

At this point (and here we quote John's own words), the 'real, arrogant, conceited and juvenile Mr Anstey would have liked to be dancing around Counsel's chambers with his hands clasped above his head like a triumphant boxer, waving to the crowd'. It appeared to those present, however, that Mr Anstey sat modestly upon hearing this decision, 'his features revealing no hint of satisfaction or triumph'. Perhaps as he sat there he remembered the occasions on which he had been just as thumpingly wrong.

Lance too has had occasions in conferences with eminent Counsel where they have quickly propounded a certain view and changed it after listening to his own views on the subject. However, he admits that those occasions have been few and far between, and although he confesses to having felt a little smug about it once or twice in years gone by, his years of experience since have rather tempered his confidence.

Another kind of ambiguity is sometimes found in deeds which attempt to reserve certain rights to vendors or lessors: and these are not just isolated incidences. More than once John and Lance have met clauses which began by reserving the right for the vendor to build anything he wanted on his retained land, regardless of its effect upon the light and air of the land disposed of, and ended by saying that he could do so provided he didn't injure the light and air of the buildings on that land. What do such clauses mean? The authors must confess that they have not the faintest idea. A lady is supposed to have asked the poet Browning what a certain poem meant, and he replied: 'Madam, when I wrote that poem, only God and Robert Browning understood it. Now only God does'. Much the same seems to be true of those who cobbled together such contradictory deeds.

There are two morals to this chapter. The first is to read all deeds and relevant plans with the utmost care to see into which category they fall. The second is to try to ensure that any deeds into which you have any input are expressed with unambiguous clarity.

Trees
(and the like)

At the time of commencing the drafting of this revised edition Lance was anticipating clarification of the position by means of the long-awaited and much-debated High Hedges Bill, which most people were expecting to come into force during 2005. However, having held off finalisation of this chapter waiting for the High Hedges Bill, the blighters – whoever they are – withdrew it and in its place we have the *Anti-social Behaviour Act* 2003 (the 2003 Act), which came into force on 1 June 2005 and incorporates many of the originally proposed provisions from the High Hedges Bill.

The best way of merging a new section on the new 2003 Act with John Anstey's original Chapter 7 was to explore the impact of the new 2003 Act first and then to reconsider John Anstey's original thoughts at the end of this new revised chapter.

The 'high hedges' element of the 2003 Act is in Part 8 and an executive summary of Part 8 would illustrate immediate concern as to its practicality. Nevertheless, the provisions are explored in a little more detail below.

High Hedges

Part 8 deals with high hedges and two of the first key things to note are that it only relates to domestic property and it deals with the impact of high hedges upon not just dwellings themselves, but also 'a garden or yard that is used and enjoyed wholly or mainly in connection with a dwelling'. It is not entirely surprising that Part 8 relates to residential properties rather than commercial properties, but the law in general covers both residential and commercial properties alike. It is perhaps more interesting to note that Part 8 attempts to deal with gardens and amenity spaces, because although that is a relevant provision with regard to Town and Country Planning, the law on rights of light has only ever related to rights of light to buildings through defined apertures.

Perhaps the most confusing part about the introductory section of Part 8 relates to the description of a 'high hedge'. It is said to mean 'so much of a barrier to light or access' and the reader is immediately left to wonder where access comes into it. One often refers to something – commonly a building – obstructing the access to light to a neighbouring property, but how does that fit into this particular description? At the time of drafting this chapter Lance had not managed to get to the bottom of, but he hopes to do so before too long.

This description of a high hedge is then extended to confirm that it is a barrier to light which '(a) is formed wholly or predominantly by a line of two or more evergreens; and (b) rises to a height of more than two metres above ground level'. That is all very well, but what if the evergreens are not in distinct lines, but in some other pattern that still forms an obstruction. Hopefully the reference to 'a line' will not be enforced too literally. Another problem is that depending upon its proximity to a garden and/or the windows of a dwelling, a hedge to a height of two metres could still create a problem. However, although this is a very general approach, it would probably be impractical to try to deal with all eventualities, because one could then get into complicated equations dealing with height, distance from the obstruction, orientation, etc. Perhaps this is an early pointer to the fact that Part 8 is only intended as a rather general guide for domestic situations, therefore avoiding too many intricacies or mathematical equations.

Any complaint regarding the impact of a high hedge is to be made to the relevant Local Authority and it is important to note that the Local Authority itself decides the merits of the complaint and what, if any, action it requires to be taken by the owner of the 'neighbouring property'. Note here that the neighbouring property is the property on which the offending high hedge is situated.

Sensibly, in the first instance the Local Authority has to consider whether the complainant has taken all reasonable steps to resolve the matters complained of prior to registering an official complaint. If the complainant fails to do so or the Local Authority resolves that the complaint is 'frivolous or vexatious' they must notify all relevant parties of their decision that the complaint should not be proceeded with. If, on the other hand, it is felt that the complaint has some merit, the Local Authority can issue a remedial notice specifying what remedial measures they require to be taken or, in the event of non compliance, access the neighbouring property and implement the works themselves, thereafter recovering the cost.

In giving notice of its decision, the Local Authority must specify its reasons, and all relevant parties in respect of the neighbouring land and the complainant's land have a right of appeal to the Secretary of State (for England) and the National Assembly for Wales (in Wales).

This poses two questions – perhaps better described as concerns – relating to Part 8, as follows:

1. How does the Local Authority determine whether the offending high hedge requires remedial action and, if so, to what extent?

    The intention is perhaps to authorise the Local Authority to exercise reasonable judgment, but that is terribly subjective and almost bound to lead to further disputes and numerous appeals. When dealing with the impact upon light to a building, one alternative would be to judge the position on the basis of what would constitute an actionable loss of light in common law. However, that would require the Local Authority to have a proper understanding of the law and that in itself is not practical. They could employ the services of a rights of light consultant, but the cost might well be prohibitive and overcomplicate the issue. Another alternative would be to assess the impact upon the windows to dwellings and gardens by reference to the guidance provided in the BRE document 'Site Layout Planning for Daylight and Sunlight: A Guide to Good Practice'. That is relevant to Town and Country Planning and therefore might more easily be adopted by a Local Authority when acting under the provisions of Part 8, but the BRE guide does not provide hard and fast rules and, once again, would probably make the matter rather more complicated than the 2003 Act envisages.

2. What impact might Part 8 have upon the normal common law rights of parties in respect of rights of light?

    As John Anstey explained, there is very little case law relating to trees and the question of light, but, generally, it is accepted that trees can form an obstruction giving rise to a right of action in law in respect of nuisance. Therefore one wonders whether compliance with a remedial notice under Part 8 would be a good defence in law.

When giving evidence in a recent court case his opponent suggested Lance was in the minority in believing that trees are a relevant consideration and could lead to a right of action in isolation. Lance is far from convinced that he is in the minority, but even if that were so he remains confident that the majority would be wrong!

Unsurprisingly, only the more interesting parts of the 2003 Act have been picked out for discussion, setting aside many pages of procedural detail including withdrawal or relaxation of notices, the detailed appeal procedure, powers of entry, powers of enforcement, etc. It is all both relevant and important, but perhaps not worthy of detailed explanation in this simple review.

While the law does deal with the impact of trees upon light to buildings and provide suitable remedies in the event of actionable infringements, Part 8 might assist in dealing with relatively small – not necessarily simple – disputes between neighbours that would otherwise end up in lengthy and costly litigation. Lance still has reservations about what he might rudely describe as the rather woolly nature of some of the terminology, which in itself could lead to dispute and numerous appeals, but it might just provide a workable and common sense resolution to what are sometimes quite minor issues.

Where Part 8 certainly could assist is with regard to the impact of high hedges upon gardens and amenity spaces. The planning process in general, and the BRE guide in particular, deal with the question of overshadowing to some extent, but only in connection with new developments or works of extension, whereas fast growing evergreens such as the now infamous leylandii, can quickly produce an anti-social and totally unnecessary degree of overshadowing of adjacent land.

Unable to see the wood for the trees?

In the previous edition of this book John Anstey stated that the position with trees in the rights of light world was far from clear and Lance agrees that this still remains the case. John cited the case of *Metaxides v Adamson*, 1971, where it was held that to grow a screen of greenery right outside a window which had just been allowed to be opened was derogation from grant – but the planting followed hard upon the openings in this case. John stressed that no one he knew of had been taken to court because of the slow and natural growth of plants, and admitted to uncertainty in his own mind as to whether courts would treat deciduous and evergreen trees identically.

Like John, Lance has been called in to give an opinion on a number of cases involving trees – but has not yet had one go before a court. While from a professional standpoint he considers it his job to keep people out of court wherever possible, and thus should be happy about this lack of activity in respect of trees, he admits that from a personal point of view, and for interest's sake, a nice juicy court case would be welcome. All the authors can do therefore in this chapter is to tell you about some of their undecided cases, and how they might have turned out.

Perhaps the most interesting of John's cases in this respect involved a new town. One of the residential areas had been carved out of a wood, and within that wood stood a very ancient cottage. Some trees were included in the gardens of the new houses and, after a while, the owner of the cottage sued the owner of one house on the grounds that, since he had owned that house, the trees in the garden had grown to such an extent that they injured the cottage's light. John's evidence (backed by an arboricultural colleague) was going to be that the effect, if any, of the alleged growth was small, and that over the centuries, particular trees might grow and die, but the general height and density of the wood was likely to remain much the same. The suit was dropped. However, this does not help us much, as in other cases trees definitely do cause a significant loss of light and may grow to create a problem in the future if the nuisance is not abated.

In another case, John's client was offended by the growth of a thick evergreen hedge outside her kitchen window. There was no doubt that her light was being affected, but the problem was solved when the neighbour was persuaded to trim – and promise to keep trimmed – the hedge to a reasonable height. This case introduces the two possibilities raised in the final sentence of the paragraph above, and which warrant more detailed consideration.

Let us deal firstly with what seems to be the simpler of the two points, namely whether trees can cause a serious loss of light. Lance believes that the answer must be 'yes', and has little doubt that a court would agree with him. However, he is also of the opinion that it makes a great deal of difference whether the trees are densely grouped so that little light can flow through them, and whether the trees are evergreen or deciduous. Where, as is not uncommon, one is dealing with a dense group of evergreens – leylandii appears to be everyone's pet hate at the moment, but there are others – they can effectively form a solid obstruction not dissimilar to that of a solid wall or building. Where one is dealing with evergreens, but they are reasonably well spaced, the situation is more complicated. However, with an accurate survey of the trees and access to a suitable computer program, it should be possible to calculate the light flowing through the gaps in the trees reasonably accurately. Yet more complicated is the situation where one is dealing with deciduous trees. When the trees are in leaf, it is very difficult indeed to assess accurately the light flowing through them; the situation is no simpler in the barren winter months when the leaves have deserted us and one must try to assess the light flowing through the remaining branches. In theory, one could perhaps model a tree with all its branches reasonably accurately on the basis of a very detailed survey and photographs, but the cost would be entirely prohibitive and even then one could argue that it did not truly represent the reality of the situation, because there would be transitional periods when the trees were only partly in leaf. What a mess! Perhaps the only answer is to lop and ban future planting of all deciduous trees and only permit evergreens to be grown – a very silly point, but it emphasises the difficulty we face in dealing with obstructions created by trees.

Assuming that we are agreed that there is the prospect of sustaining a rights of light claim in respect of obstruction by trees, Lance believes that the next and potentially even more difficult problem is how the law caters for the fact that trees – unlike buildings – have a nasty habit of growing of their own accord. Although buildings can be extended and increased in height, one needs to obtain certain permissions in advance and the affected neighbour can not only see the problem developing, but can go to court and prove what the impact upon his light will be. Trees, on the other hand, proceed with greater stealth, generally – the authors admit that there are exceptions – growing very slowly, so that the interference with light takes place by degrees over a period of time. Bearing in mind the position with rights of light acquired by prescription, could that mean that the affected party loses its right to object if it does not do so, and take appropriate legal steps, within a year of the interference arising?

Taking all of the above into account, it seems to Lance that trees and buildings have to be treated slightly differently. Perhaps the most logical way of dealing with trees would be for neighbours to agree upon a sensible height, and further agree that they should be lopped or pruned on a six-monthly, or similar, basis, to avoid a problem arising. Following that through, if the parties cannot agree – neighbours seem to like to go to war over such matters – a court could make a declaration confirming the maximum height the offending trees could grow to and make an order for them to be lopped or pruned on certain dates. At least then the offended neighbour would have something to enforce if his neighbour transgressed. That may seem quite simple, but life rarely is, and trees are no exception. For example, one might need the advice of an arboriculturalist as to how quickly and how densely a tree or hedge is likely to grow.

Where one is dealing with foliage immediately adjacent to a boundary, the neighbour could, to some extent, deal with the matter himself by cutting back any offending parts overhanging the boundary, because that is his common law right. However, the parts of the tree or hedge causing the problem might be beyond the line of the boundary by a fraction – or be yet more distant, in which case to cut them down would probably involve an act of trespass. (Those readers particularly interested in boundaries are directed to the new edition of *Anstey's Boundary Disputes* – a sister publication to this one, updated in 2004 by David Powell.)

Tree Preservation Orders

On a slightly different tack, but still on trees, beware of tree preservation orders (TPOs). Even your own trees can affect your light, of course, and you may be prohibited from pruning even them.

Let's finish with one last undecided case. John had a client who had some limes at the pavement side of her front garden, which was a mere 20 feet or so in length. Every year for 30 or 40 years these limes had been pollarded so that there was adequate light in the winter to the front room. When a TPO was made on all the trees in the street, John's client raised no objection – indeed, she was all in favour. However, when she had the limes pollarded as usual, the council threatened her with imprisonment, or a substantial fine at the very least. John was asked, and was able, to give evidence that the living room would have been plunged into Stygian gloom if the limes had been allowed to grow unchecked. A satisfactory accommodation was thus arrived at.

8 Abandonment

No one knows what constitutes abandonment, that is to say, giving up a right which you have acquired – not even your omniscient original author (John) and Lance. It is a matter of the facts in each case, or as John used to say, what the judge had for breakfast. That remark was not quite as lighthearted as it may have seemed; nor was it intended as a jibe at judges. John was simply pointing out that it is a grey area, part based upon facts and part based upon opinions. (John himself confessed that there were a number of matters about which his own opinion fluctuated according to whether there was an 'r' in the month: for example about God and creation. He said that half the time he thought the world was so complicated that only God could have created it; the other half of the time that it was so complicated that not even God could have devised it. Lance shares his confusion on that and many other matters besides.)

Under the circumstances then, one can only provide guidelines as to what definitely does and what definitely does not constitute abandonment, leaving the grey area for us all to ponder.

A mere temporary failure to use light certainly does not lose the right. On the basis of the ruling in *Tehidy*

Minerals Ltd v Norman, 1971, the necessary criteria for abandonment of an easement were considered and confirmed as 'a fixed intention never at any time thereafter to assert the right himself or to attempt to transmit it to anyone else'. We can therefore be certain – or at least as certain as one ever can be about anything in law – that a temporary failure to use light will not lead to the legal right being lost; there must be a clear intention to no longer use and rely upon that right at all.

In Lance's opinion, perhaps the key factor is the manner in which a window has been blocked. However, a court is also likely to consider timing – for how long the blocking-up of a window has continued – and any inferences that can be drawn from the actions of the parties over the relevant period. In addition – and potentially very importantly – the courts are likely also to consider whether the owner of the servient land has relied upon the actions of his neighbour; for example, by proceeding to build and obstruct the original 'openings' on the assumption that the light had been abandoned and was no longer being used.

There are two very interesting examples of case law on abandonment, one presuming it, the other rebutting it. In the first of these, *Moore v Rawson*, 1824, a chap pulled down his wall, which had windows in it, and rebuilt it imperforate. When another chap came along and put a building near the wall, the first chap started putting windows in again, and brought an action against the latter builder for obstruction. He lost and, the authors would argue, deservedly so. It is their understanding that the decision was at least partly based on the fact that the defendant had assumed abandonment of the windows and therefore not unreasonably built without reference to the alleged rights of the plaintiff.

In the other case, *Kino v The Ecclesiastical Commissioners*, 1880, a church was pulled down and the site was going to be sold, so some poor innocent put up a building next to the vacant site. Much to John's surprise – and to the poor innocent's, no doubt – the Church Commissioners succeeded in their action against him. This case serves to show how careful one has to be when confronted by a cleared site – and the importance of researching its history. John correctly pointed out that as a matter of fact it is often quite difficult actionably to injure light to churches, as they are generally lit from various directions. He also proffered the suggestion that when points of law are decided in cases involving churches, the facts of the actual injury are very often barely considered – but Lance is not sure he would entirely agree with him in that respect.

In general, where the means of blocking up the windows is of a clearly temporary nature – in one case that the authors know of, involving piles of shoe boxes – it is highly unlikely that abandonment would arise even if it were over an extended period. Lance would generally take the same view with regard to the boarding-up of windows – often done for security purposes based upon the current building use – but would express that view guardedly, on the basis of the decision in *Smith v Baxter,* 1990, where the boarding-up of windows over a lengthy period was deemed to constitute abandonment. Most often, the question which the practitioner will have to consider will relate to bricked-up (bricks or blocks) windows. It seems, from the leading cases, that the courts would want to be convinced of the dominant owner's clear intention to abandon his rights in bricking-up the windows. On the basis of the ruling in *Marine and General Mutual Life Assurance Society v St James' Real*

Estate Co Ltd, 1991, an important factor will be the state of the brick reveals. If the joints have been broken in the closing such that the brick infill is bonded into the surrounding brickwork, the court is reasonably likely to conclude that the window has been abandoned. However, if the reveals are left straight-jointed, such that the infill panel could easily be removed in the future, it is more likely that a court would consider it a temporary measure.

Figure 1: Broken reveals, with brick infill bonded into the wall, indicate that there is probably no intention ever to use the window again

A puzzling case with which John once had to deal had a very gratifying ending for him. A client was proposing a development alongside a building (John recalled this as being an ice-cream factory), which had a number of lofty windows facing towards the site. They were going to be so badly affected that John recommended a direct approach to the dominant owner. 'But the windows have been abandoned', protested the architect, 'They're completely blocked by breeze-block walls inside.' John

Figure 2: Straight reveals, and a brick infilling panel, indicate that there may be an intention to reopen the window at some future date

replied that he thought that they did not count as abandoned, and that the walls had probably been put there while the site was a prey to vandals. 'Mark my words', he said, 'When your building goes up, the breeze blocks will come down.' Several years later he was relating this case, while talking about abandonment, to a Society of Architects in the same borough as the development. He told them he did not know whether his words had come true. A man then stood up in the audience and said: 'You obviously don't recognise me, but I was the architect on that job. The walls came down, and the windows are now being used'.

As mentioned earlier, time comes into the equation as well. This is particularly true when we are talking about abandoning a right, rather than abandoning an actual window. Whereas interruption for a year (physical or by the theoretical device of the notional obstruction) is sufficient to defeat a claim under the *Prescription Act*, an action under a lost grant or time immemorial will lie for rather longer. Arguably, in fact, it will lie for six years, having regard to the Statute of Limitations, although John received advice from two distinguished firms of solicitors, who strongly argued that it was not a question of a single course of action, and that therefore the limitation period did not apply. The solicitors' view was that a breach of one's easement is a continuing nuisance, and the question as to whether one has abandoned one's right or not is thus a matter of fact and degree for the court every time. However, Lance, like John, while noting the point made, finds it hard to believe a court would entertain a claim for loss of light that occurred more than six years ago.

The authors would hope that the above passages provide useful guidance – but acknowledge that they do not provide a great deal in the way of certainty. Windows that have been bricked up on a toothed and bonded reveal basis over an extended period are almost certain to be deemed abandoned, but with anything short of that, there is less certainty, and a developer must act with caution. If in doubt, one might seek Counsel's opinion – and it may also be sensible to at least notify the affected neighbour of your intentions, even if you do not want to go as far as directly opening discussions on the question of abandonment.

To add to the confusion, all of the above relates to abandonment of a prescriptive right, but what about the non-continuous user? Lance's understanding – based upon specialist legal advice – is that if someone has temporarily blocked his windows for security or other reasons with boarding or something similarly easy to remove, while he may not have abandoned his right, he is susceptible to the argument that he cannot pursue a claim on the basis of prescriptive rights because he cannot show 20 years continuous use. If so, he may then have to revert to lost modern grant and whatever complications that may bring. Therefore, think very carefully before blocking your own light, even if you do so only as a temporary measure.

9 Alterations

Shakespeare said: 'Love is not love, which alters when it alteration finds', and to a great extent the same is true of light and the right to it. Your right to light is to receive light through a defined aperture; it is not just a general right to all the light and air that may happen to be floating about over the next-door field, or whatever. Indeed, it was John's opinion that the law had gone rather further than it might have done in accommodating changes in windows.

In effect, there are two different forms of alteration to a building that are relevant to rights of light. The first relates to the alteration of window openings and the second to alterations to the internal arrangements and partitioning within the dominant tenement. In fact, the two overlap in some cases, for example, where a building is demolished and replaced by a new building with slightly different sized windows in a slightly different position in a room with slightly different floor levels and room sizes.

John suggested that most leading cases are confusing largely because the courts do not really understand the science of light. That may be true in part, but Lance would like to think that most rights of light consultants at least understand the science of light, and yet they seem to be equally uncertain on the subject and, at times, very much divided as to what is the correct legal interpretation of any particular situation.

Alteration of window openings

Obviously, if you enlarge a window you are not making things more difficult for the servient owner, because the law revolves around assessing whether the injured room will be left adequately lit, and clearly, the larger the window opening serving it, the easier it is to leave it adequately lit. It therefore follows that if a chap is going to cause an actionable obstruction to your new, larger window, he would certainly have caused an actionable injury to the original opening. It also follows that if you make your windows smaller – less likely, but still possible – you may be imposing an additional burden on the chap next door and, although the case law is not entirely clear on this point, you would be unlikely to succeed in an action unless you could prove that the old, larger windows would have been injured just as much as the new, smaller ones.

When you are dealing with the same sized windows, but just shifting them about a bit, John always thought that one could rely on the words of Farwell J in *News of the World Ltd v Allen Fairhead & Sons Ltd*, 1931. In this case, the judge tried to apply the test of nuisance laid down in *Higgins v Betts*, 1905, to a case where there was very little coincidence of windows. His important paragraph began with the words used by all judges when there has been a lot of argument about the law, and they are about to reject one perfectly reasonable side of it: 'The true view is this' (in other words, 'I think'). Unless the injury to the small coincident bit of window is in itself enough to amount to an actionable injury, the dominant owner cannot restrain the servient owner from building.

A more helpful case is one in which a wall had swung through a slight angle, so that the change in its position varied from one foot to two feet five inches. The Court of Appeal concurred in holding that the right had not been abandoned by moving the wall. It therefore seems, if only as an approximate rule of thumb, that you are probably safe if you move the plane of your window wall by a foot – and possibly still all right if it is by three to four feet – but beyond that you could be in difficulty.

A general rule is to keep in mind the idea of congruent triangles. If all the angles and all the sides are equal, triangles are congruent. It's the same with windows: the closer everything is to how it was before, in size, shape, position, plane, and even as to numbers and relation to the other parts of the building and other windows, the easier it is going to be to prove identity of burden. No congruity, no continuity of right. In order to prove the identity, it is a very good idea to keep a reliable record, both photographic and surveyed, of the former apertures.

Internal alterations

The question of internal alterations is a bit more tricky. John always thought, but admitted that he was not sure if the law supported him, that one was only entitled to light to areas which had been lit for the prescriptive period. This seems a sensible approach to Lance. In other words, you can't suddenly enlarge your room and thus increase the burden on the servient owner so that when he builds, one year later, an extension which would not have actionably injured the light to your room in its earlier state, now forms the basis of a claim against him.

John's view was that the use to which a man has chosen to put his light neither increases nor diminishes his right, so that whether he is temporarily using the boardroom as a cleaners' cupboard or vice versa is irrelevant. However, if he physically alters the layout of his premises, it can substantially affect the position of the servient owner. Lance would certainly agree with the latter point, but would argue that the use to which a room is put is also important. While he is sure that a court would and should consider possible future uses, it has to be realistic. Therefore, if the only serious impact upon an office building was to a series of WC cubicles and an associated washroom area, it seems unlikely that a court would accept an argument that this could be converted to the main boardroom at some point in the future, making the loss of light that much more critical and thus worthy of an injunction. (In truth, Lance does not think that John would have taken his point to this extreme either, but simply emphasises the fact that one has to be careful and sensible when considering current and possible future uses.)

With regard to changes in room shape and sizes, let us take two simple examples to illustrate these. In the first, a room is 12 feet deep from the window, by 10 feet wide, all well lit. A building is erected opposite which would limit the adequate lighting to seven feet deep into the room. In the original state of that room, no actionable injury would be suffered. Suppose, though, that just prior to the building opposite being erected, the dominant

Figure 3: If the partition is taken away, for 20 years to come, only the effect on the front area has to be considered if a new building is erected opposite

owner knocks down the back wall of his room and makes it 20 feet deep (see Figure 3). The same effect on the lighting by the same building would now produce an actionably injured room. It surely cannot be right that, without prescribing for it, the servient owner can suddenly make life much more difficult for the dominant owner.

In the second example, the case is reversed. A 20-foot-deep room is partitioned (more or less permanently) so that it is now only 12 feet deep (see Figure 4). Can the dominant owner now claim that the servient owner's building has injured his prescriptive light? John argued not, stating that he had abandoned the right to light to the larger room by building the partition.

While Lance understands John's logic and feels there is merit in his argument, he does not feel it is a cut and dry

Figure 4.

case. All that can really be said is that the law is not altogether clear on these points. The authors have therefore given their understanding of the position, indicating both their own uncertainty and dare they say it, slight confusion. A well-argued court case thoroughly examining all of the various complications that can arise, some of these set out above, would certainly be welcome. Even so, quite a few cases involving some of these subtle alterations of the dominant tenement would be likely to end with the judge giving his 'true view'.

Conclusion

Lance's conclusion is that a court is likely to look at what is fair and reasonable in all the circumstances – British justice at its best! On the one hand, it seems well established that a man is entitled to use his property as he wishes and should not be tied to a particular arrangement to accommodate works of extension or development on his neighbour's land. On the other hand, a balance has to be struck to ensure that potential future uses, layouts, etc. are both practical and do not unreasonably increase the burden upon a neighbour to provide light from a particular source.

10 Remedies

The basic right of anyone who has established a right to light is to retain the light to a minimum standard (that is, what the law considers adequate). Originally, there were no two ways about it. If your light was injured by a new building or a redevelopment, you got an injunction restraining the development, or having it pulled down; and if you couldn't prove an injury, you lost your action and the building continued.

In *Anstey's Party Walls* (recently updated by Graham North), John mentioned with approval certain ancient writings, and they are just as relevant and interesting on the subject of rights of light today. Vitruvius, who wrote around the year dot, plus or minus 50 years, gave a very good basic rule for establishing whether an injury has been suffered, concentrating correctly on whether there has been a loss of sky visibility. A ninth-century Byzantine emperor, Theophilus, is recorded as hearing a rights of light claim against his wife's brother, Petronas, whose palace extension was blocking out an old lady's light. Her right was upheld and Petronas was publicly flogged. I dare say that some dominant owners would like to see such a penalty brought back into use. A book published by the London Record Society, part-edited by John's former history tutor Dr Helena Chew, deals with the London Assize of Nuisance, 1301–1401, and gives details of several rights of light cases. For example, in 1341 Geoffrey Aleyn complained that the parson of St Stephen's, Walbrook, had obscured windows for which there was a right to light. He satisfied the mayor and the sheriffs as to his right, and the defendants were ordered to remove the impediment within 40 days. By contrast, in 1343 Rose de Farndon complained that Hugh de Brandon was building so as to obscure the light which she had enjoyed across a street called Goderom Lane for 'time out of mind'. Hugh proved that the land had always been built on, and so Rose lost her action.

Some history

Matters went on being decided in a similar way for many years, by which time many people had come to think that there were some cases in which an injunction was altogether too dramatic a remedy to deal with small injuries, at least in the courts of equity. In common law it had been possible to obtain damages, but plaintiffs didn't always know or choose the correct channel for their actions, and could be referred from one court to another. The *Chancery Amendment Act* of 1858, usually known as *Lord Cairns' Act*, duly gave the Court of Chancery the power to award damages in lieu of an injunction, if it seemed equitable to them so to do. (This has now been superseded by section 50 of the *Supreme Court Act 1981*.)

The four tests

The way in which the courts should address themselves to the question of an injunction or damages was much

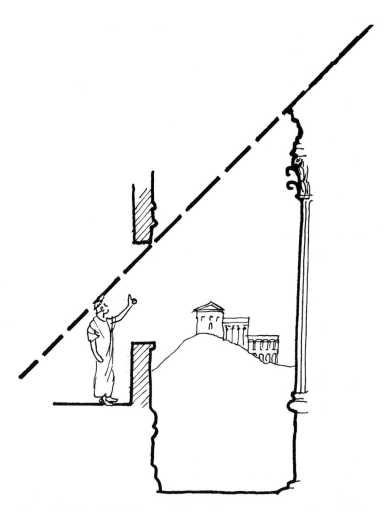

Figure 5: Vitruvius had a good idea of how to assess a rights of light injury, and gives this Corinthian building the thumbs up

clarified by *Shelfer v City of London Electric Lighting Co*, 1895, in which four tests were laid down to be applied. They were, and are:

1. Is the injury small?
2. Is it one which can be estimated in money?

3. Would a small money payment be an adequate remedy?
4. Would it be oppressive to the defendant to grant an injunction?

Two of these questions are easy to answer, one difficult, and one impossible. Let's deal with the easy ones first.

A question of money

It is fairly easy to estimate most losses of light in money terms. John admitted that he might have difficulty measuring the value of an effect upon a notable stained glass window in a cathedral (he did actually have a case that necessitated this), but he reckoned to be able to cope with most domestic and commercial cases – and even some ecclesiastical ones. You, the reader, will be given some advice on how to do so in Chapter 12, on valuation. There is certainly scope for debate, particularly with regard to residential properties.

Oppression of the defendant

It is, perhaps, more straightforward to decide whether the defendant would be harshly treated by an injunction. If he has acted openly, and the plaintiff has watched his progress without a word of complaint, and then seized the most damaging time to bring an action for an injunction in the hope of being bought off with a considerable bribe, then the plaintiff is not likely to win the sympathy of the courts. If, on the other hand, the defendant has tried to keep the plaintiff as much in the dark as he can, while the plaintiff has protested at the earliest possible moment, an injunction is far more likely to be awarded.

Linked to this, the court will also have to consider the ramifications, for the defendant, of being stopped at a late and critical stage – they might be tied into building contracts or have already agreed the sale of new apartments, for example.

An adequate remedy?

Now we come to the difficult one: is a small money payment an adequate remedy? The question is easier with commercial properties than domestic ones, but not entirely straightforward with either. John Anstey felt that as the owner of a commercial building you were arguably no worse off if the residual value of your property combined with the compensation paid amounted to no less than the original value of the property before the light was taken away. However, while that may be a sound approach for a freeholder simply looking at the property as an investment, that might not be the same for the occupier who might put greater emphasis on the importance of good light conditions; indeed it may have been quite a significant deciding factor when the occupier was considering which premises to rent. Lance is particularly interested in the reference to a 'small' money payment, because he is not quite sure how to assess what is small in the context of the building's value and, yet more importantly, he is far from convinced that this is the way courts now view the situation when considering injunction applications. The recent *Midtown* case is a prime example, because while an injunction was not granted we can be fairly certain that the compensation sum awarded is likely to be reasonably substantial and may even relate to a share of the developer's profit. The point being made is that while the tests in the *Shelfer* case are still relevant, in certain circumstances – particularly large office buildings – it is highly likely that a court will award damages in certain circumstances even if the resultant compensation award is large rather than small.

Is the injury small?

Now to the impossible bit; in a house or flat, the answer may depend upon what room or rooms are affected. Roughly, in order of lighting importance, the authors would say that the rooms of a house are: living room, kitchen, dining room, bedroom, bathroom. If you live in a house grand enough to have more elaborate rooms such as a ballroom or a library, then you can afford to consult Lance personally as to where those rooms rank. If the injury is a serious one to either of the first two rooms, it seems certain that test number 3 has failed, and if it is to either of the last two, it might well be passed. To the middle one, the authors would argue that it could be more seriously injured than a living room and still pass, but couldn't take as severe a blow as a bedroom. A family room/breakfast room is half living room and half kitchen, and behaves accordingly.

It is impossible to know what is meant by small, and neither Lance nor John has ever come across any cases in which the matter has been specifically considered. John related that his father once asked an assembly of very learned lawyers what 'small' meant and, according to him, they went into a sort of huddle from which the oldest and wisest emerged, stroking his long white beard and said gravely: 'Well I should say' – dramatic pause – 'that it would not be large'.

In a large office block, if the light to one room is obliterated that can surely only be a small injury to the building as a whole. But if that room is a key office to a small firm, in the context of that firm's occupancy it could be said to be a significant injury. In addition, John pointed out that in considering a particular room one has to take account of the amount of existing light prevailing. For example, if you only have a little light to start with, even a small loss can represent a serious change for the worse. In that connection, John mentioned that his father was very fond of the image of the noose. If a man had a noose around his neck which dangles to his waist, you can take in a lot of slack without doing him any harm; but if it is already tight around his neck, one twitch might be enough to send him to eternity.

Therefore, surely 'small' must be a matter of judgment, knowing all the circumstances.

Damages v injunction: the shifting balance

On the basis of *Shelfer*, it must be emphasised that all four tests have to be passed, not just one or even the majority. Furthermore, their general tenor must always be borne in mind: if the injury is not trivial, damages are not a sufficient remedy and an injunction will lie. This was always the ruling in *Shelfer*, and Lindley, LJ said in that case that 'the court has always protested against the notion that it ought to allow a wrong to continue simply because the wrongdoer is able and willing to pay for the injury which he may inflict'. A few years later, in *Cowper v Laidler*, 1903, Buckley, J said: 'The court has affirmed over and over again that the jurisdiction to give damages ... is not so to be used as in fact to enable the defendant ... to purchase from the plaintiff against his will the legal right to the easement'.

Over the years that followed, however, it seemed to John that the see-saw had gradually tilted in favour of the defendant, and that the tests were being applied in a way that said, in effect: 'Is the injury serious? If not, the remedy is damages'. By 1984, in other words, John felt that the exact opposite of the original question was being applied, and wrote articles and papers saying so. Then came *Pugh v Howells*, however, and the Court of Appeal reaffirmed, in the strongest terms, the words of A. L. Smith, LJ in *Shelfer*, when he emphasised how reluctant the courts should be to allow the servient owner to buy himself out of his breach of the dominant owner's rights. (You should also see *Deakins v Hookings*, 1993.)

Anyone who seriously injures his neighbour's light must, in the context of these cases, put himself at grave risk of an injunction. The courts will be particularly inclined to penalise him if he has carried on in the face of vigorous protests from his neighbour, or even if it can be shown that his own advisers had counselled caution – as had happened in Pugh's case. The intending developer should therefore think very carefully about the potential cost of being stopped in his tracks by an adjoining owner. He would do well to consider, at this stage, whether or not to modify his proposed building or extension before next door – or the courts – get to hear about it. It may be that, if his architect can produce a satisfactory solution with a smaller profile, it will pay to show the larger solution to the opposition first, and allow them to 'force' the developer to cut back his scheme to the already prepared position, which may well make both sides happy – always a desirable result.

The reason that so much care must be taken in avoiding provoking an injunction is that it will, in all probability, restrict the would-be developer to an obstruction no greater than the former buildings on the site, almost

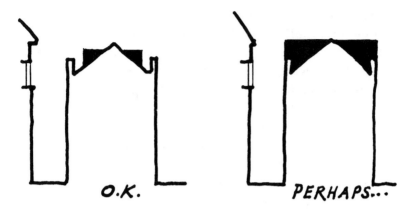

Figure 6: You should certainly build the extension shown in the first picture, and possibly the one shown in the second

Figure 7: If you tried to get away with the third, and your irate neighbour obtained an injunction, you would not be allowed to build the second and could not be absolutely confident of being able to build the first – you could, feasibly, be pushed back to where you started

certainly not much more: it will not allow him to commit a moderate injury. Since he can be fairly sure of getting away with damages for a small injury, he should consider whether it is really worth going for a much larger building which might be stopped altogether.

While these passages from the previous edition of John's book still hold good in the main, the recent *Midtown* case is a good example of how, whilst the question of injunctions – whether they are likely to be granted or not – might commence with consideration of the actual loss of light, there are other potential considerations to take account of, not least of all the actions of the parties prior to the litigation.

Risks to the dominant owner

The risks are not all on one side, however. If the dominant owner wishes to bring an action to restrain a development, having been unable to negotiate a reasonable settlement with the developer, he must consider how he is going to go about it. He will certainly express his action as being for an injunction and/or damages, but the real question he must decide is whether to go for interlocutory proceedings (see below), or to let the action take its normal course. If he chooses the latter, building is very likely to continue pending the trial of the action, and counsel for the defendants will doubtless make great play with the fact that he did not go for interlocutory relief. Despite all that we have quoted above, it is very unlikely in such circumstances that the courts will issue a mandatory order for the pulling down of a completed building, and the plaintiff will thus have to be content with money.

The threat of an injunction is, of course, a potent one, even if it is lying there waiting for a full trial of the matter. In a notorious case, *Blue Town v Higgs and Hill*, 1990, the defendants applied to have the action struck out unless the plaintiffs applied for interlocutory relief. The Court virtually acceded to this novel line of argument, but a case soon after, *Oxy Electric v Zainuddin*, 1990, cast grave doubt on the correctness of this decision, and did not follow it.

Interlocutory proceedings

It may be that some readers are not familiar with interlocutory proceedings, and we will therefore explain why the plaintiff finds himself on the horns of a beastly dilemma. If you think that your light is going to be really badly affected, and only stopping the building will save you, you can ask a judge, at short notice, to stop the work immediately (or to halt publication, or whatever your particular action is about; this isn't just true of rights of light cases). He will do so if you can make out a prima facie case and, as is usually so in building matters, the balance between the parties can best be maintained by putting everything into suspense until the full case can be tried, perhaps some months later. But – and it is a very big but – he will only do so if, normally through Counsel, you give 'the usual undertakings'.

Obviously, every plaintiff would like to stop the wicked developer in his tracks, but it is 'the usual undertakings' which deter him. If he loses his action, the plaintiff may have been forced to make good to the defendant all the costs which have been incurred through the cessation of the work – as well, of course, as the costs of the action.

The building costs will include any extras charged by the contractor for taking his men off the site and bringing them back again, any increases in material or labour costs which have arisen during the delay, and possibly interest lost on the money laid out on the site while idle. Only two classes of people – apart from those who are absolutely downright sure they are going to win – can afford to give such undertakings: the very poor, and the very rich. All in all, it may be better to go straight for an injunction and an expedited trial rather than seeking interim relief.

It can be assumed that the courts would look very closely at a case presented by someone who had not the means to honour an undertaking, before granting interlocutory relief. However, you can also be pretty sure that they would not look favourably on Counsel whose sole argument for resisting the proceedings was that the plaintiff was a small man without much financial backing. That does not mean that they would give an interlocutory injunction automatically to someone just because he could afford to pay if he was wrong.

John recalled a conference with a very able rights of light (and other matters) senior Counsel, during which he asked whether the plaintiff would always be called upon to honour his cross undertaking if he failed to win a final injunction, but was awarded damages. Counsel said that, obviously, if he got his injunction there would be no question of the undertaking: if there was clearly no case to answer or if it had been a case where damages were always going to be sufficient remedy then, in all probability, he would have to pay up; in his opinion, however, if the courts decided on balance to award damages after weighing the possibility of an injunction, the plaintiff would not have to bear the developer's costs of the delay. Apparently a short while afterwards, John Anstey was at a social occasion with the aforementioned barrister and a junior (but experienced) Counsel from the same chambers. He asked the latter whether he had any comment to make on this view of the situation, and he asked the senior Counsel what authority he had for his proposition. Drawing himself up to his full height of about six inches less than his junior, he said: 'You have my authority'. Clear and unequivocal and thus much better indeed, although potentially wrong!

John's rendition of this all important element of the law still holds good, and in Lance's opinion the judgment in cases such as *Midtown* does not mean the law has changed. That case simply serves to emphasise the fact that while the physical impact upon light is important, it is not the be all and end all when a judge considers the critical question of whether an injunction should be granted. The actions of the parties is a critical consideration and if the affected party dallies in defence of its light it could be fatal to its case and damages will have to do.

How to measure light

John once received a letter from a young surveyor who claimed to have studied for several years under George Wakefield and therefore claimed to be probably the best-qualified person in the country to measure loss of light to a building, by taking light-meter readings at various points on the face nearest an obstruction, and in the rooms behind. John replied (with customary modesty), that he was generally reckoned to be the best person in the country at measuring the loss of light in buildings, and that while he was full of admiration for George Wakefield on the subject of photographic lighting, the use of meters in legal cases was singularly ineffective. The young man was subsequently persuaded to consult a real expert.

Uselessness of meters

The reason that meters are useless should be obvious to a person experienced in photography. If you are taking photographs in England or Wales, you need to take a separate meter reading for each shot, even if it is only a few minutes since you took the last one, because the light from an English or Welsh sky changes all the time. You cannot, therefore, use a light-meter or photometer to measure the amount of light in a room before an offending construction begins, and then do the same again when it is complete, and hope to obtain comparable readings, because it is virtually impossible to be sure that you have exactly the same sky conditions to measure a 'before and after' set of daylighting circumstances. It is therefore essential to find a method of measurement which is not affected by fluctuations in the actual intensity of light received from the sky at any one moment.

Visibility matters

The amount of the sky itself which is visible from a certain point only changes when obstruction, temporary or permanent, obscures it. Clouds or bright sunlight make no difference to the sky *visibility*, and it is therefore this factor on which the science of measurement and the law have chosen to concentrate. In fact, the brightness of the sky varies by about six to one between summer and winter, but the same patch of sky will always be there, until someone puts a building in front of it.

In 1932 an International Conference on Illumination, meeting at Cambridge, calculated the amount of light available from the whole dome of sky. (If you were monarch of all you surveyed, from the centre all round to the sea – like Alexander Selkirk – you would see the whole dome of sky.) In the middle of an overcast day in winter, it amounts to '500 foot candles' – that is, the equivalent of 500 standard candles one foot away from the object, or as we would say today, 500 lumens. It was also decided (and presumably by this same Conference) that one lumen was adequate light to do work involving visual discrimination, and that light should be measured at the working plane. It is these supplementary decisions that make the whole system work.

Figure 8: Sunny or cloudy, winter or summer rain, hail or shine, the patch of sky visible through a window remains the same, even though its brightness may change – unless someone shoves a building up there

The 0.2% sky factor

While there have been cases where the judge has questioned whether 0.2% sky factor is a truly adequate standard, particularly in a residential circumstance, it is still the basis upon which rights of light technical assessments and calculations are based. Until such time as the approach of the courts is changed and any different standard applied, Lance continues to advise his clients on that basis. However, he has personal reservations as to whether it is an adequate standard for all occasions and, as shall be explained later, at a recent daylight conference he attended organised by the Chartered Institute of Building Services Engineers (CIBSE) some interesting points were raised on the subject by reference to a recently published paper by Paul Chynoweth.

It follows mathematically from the above that if one five-hundredth of the whole dome of sky can be seen from a point on the working plane, then at that point you have one lumen: enough light to read the small print of *The Times* (even in its tabloid version). One five-hundredth may also be expressed as 0.2%, and this is the way in which you will usually meet it. By drawing a line between a number of similar points, you will obtain a 0.2% contour. Everywhere on the working plane between that line and the window will receive at least one lumen; everywhere behind it will receive less. You will always need to draw two contours. The first contour will be of the 0.2% sky factor as it is, or was in the prescriptive conditions, before building activity started on the servient tenement, and the second contour will show the condition now that that construction has taken place, or what it is expected to be when the building is complete. By measuring the movement from one contour to the other, you can estimate the effect of the change.

As referred to above, Lance attended a recent daylighting workshop arranged by CIBSE where he and other current rights of light consultants were invited to attend and to speak on a topic of their choice. As it so happens they grouped together to set out their views on the *Midtown* case and its relevance to future consideration of daylighting conditions in office environments, but two interesting points arose from a presentation by a CIBSE member at the end of the gathering. First, reference was made to a recently published paper by Paul Chynoweth (a lecturer at Salford University) which investigates the origins of the 0.2% sky factor standard arising out of the work of Percy Waldram, in particular whether it really is an appropriate standard and was the result of full and proper research in the first instance. Secondly, whether the whole basis of the Waldram diagram approach is in itself flawed and inappropriate. However, Lance considers that these issues were rather inappropriately presented by the CIBSE member who seemed less interested in reasoned argument and much more interested in trying to prove that all rights of light consultants have been barking up the wrong tree for many years, but it is certainly worthy of further comment.

Taking the second point first, while there are different ways of assessing daylight – setting aside the Waldram diagram approach, the BRE guide alone provides three different daylight tests – for common law purposes Lance sees no reason to move away from the Waldram diagram method and the use of sky factor contours. It is an effective way of comparing existing and proposed conditions in order to assess the impact and acceptability of works of extension/redevelopment of neighbouring land, and provides us with a means of representing the situation on drawings in a form that is readily understandable. Lance recalls how the man who spoke at the CIBSE meeting was very keen to promote his own method and seemed very excited by his ability to accurately assess factors such as external reflection of neighbouring properties. As one or two people tried to point out, the law very sensibly ignores this form of reflected light because the owner of the neighbouring properties in question may demolish his building and rebuild in a completely different form and with different materials in the future, thus changing the calculations in a manner beyond the control of his other neighbours. Of more interest is Paul Chynoweth's challenge of the 0.2% sky factor target. As Lance has already mentioned, he has long held the view that 0.2% represents quite a grim standard and does foresee the possibility of a future court case reinforcing the argument that a higher standard might be appropriate for some residential situations at least. However, Paul Chynoweth suggests that an appropriate standard might be nearer to 2%. That is all very well and we would all like to see super light conditions in all buildings. However, increasing the standard of accuracy markedly in this way would give rise to significant practical difficulties. In an urban environment one would probably find that this revised sky factor value were not achieved over 50% of a room's area in most existing conditions, such that even small changes in a skyline would give rise to actionable losses. That is of course the situation with the law as it currently stands, but if one raises the bar it might stymie the proper regeneration and enhancement of urban areas to an unacceptable and inappropriate extent.

The 50/50 rule (again)

We explained in Chapter 1 on 'What is a right to light?' that, as a general rule, if 50% of the working plane in a room still receives 0.2%, or adequacy, after a development, the light to that room is generally considered not to be actionably injured. In order to make this chapter complete in itself, we can repeat the explanation about the 50/50 rule here. The test we've just outlined was accepted for many years as being almost absolute: certainly practitioners treated it that way. If 50% was still well lit, there was no injury. In the case of *Ough v King*, 1967, however, the judge relied on a view and, not being trained to judge light, decided that a room just over 50% adequately lit was nevertheless injured. Judge Cooke suggested that the 50/50 test should not be applied slavishly as it represented a bare minimum. John was always severely critical of this decision, believing that the judge made his inspection at a time when any room would have seemed dark, and that he was not capable of imagining what the light would have been like at some other time, in some other season, or in some other circumstances. Furthermore, John felt that he was substituting uncertainty for certainty, and whereas before that case a consultant, if he had done his measurement accurately, could advise a client with confidence that a building had either been injured or not, from that point onwards, no one could be absolutely sure about anything.

In the opinion of most experts, however, the 50/50 rule is still a good working guide, and can safely be adopted for commercial cases. In domestic cases you can be sure that less than 50% adequacy is an injury, pretty sure that over 55% is not, and worry about it in between. That 'worry' is the big difficulty in residential jobs.

The test of an injury is not how much is taken, but how much remains: that is why there is so much emphasis on the dividing line between an adequately and an inadequately lit room. It is once you step over that line that things start to happen. That is why it is so irritating not to have a definite line to measure, but to have to utter words of warning, like 'If one accepts the 50/50 rule, but remembering *Ough v King* ...'. While there are questions of fact and degree in each case, and one could not expect a hard and fast rule to be laid down on such a delicate subject, many experts in this field would like to see the courts set a fixed standard for injurious or non-injurious affection, so that consultants could give definite advice to clients, one way or the other. From Lance's perspective, while in theory that would provide a neat solution it would deny us the ability to assess each circumstance on its individual merits; sometimes a vital ingredient in good decision making.

Is an injury injunctable?

After an injury is known to exist – to one party at least – then it is a question of whether the appropriate remedy is an injunction or damages. Advising on whether an injury is injunctable is the most difficult task that the rights of light consultant has to undertake during the course of a job. Carrying out the Waldram diagram calculations (to which you will be introduced in a couple of pages' time) may be time-consuming and is certainly not easy until you get the hang of it, but the value judgment on 'injunctability' is extremely tricky and if you get it wrong you will possibly ruin your client – and perhaps yourself as well. This is certainly true if you are acting for the developer. Acting for the injured party is a lot easier. And of course, you can always tell the developer that you are going to seek an injunction, and then leave *his* consultant to worry about your chances. John related much of his comments to the manual method of assessment, whereas we now have computer software that makes the technical element that much easier.

The chapter on remedies (Chapter 10) goes into more detail about the likelihood of an injunction or damages, while that on valuation (Chapter 12) explains how the different amounts of injury are assessed in money terms. In this chapter we are only concerned with actually measuring the effect in physical terms.

The 45° rule

It is regrettably still necessary to say a word or two on the so-called 45° rule. Despite all of John's efforts, and indeed, those of his father before him, the rule still seems to be alive and kicking in certain people's minds. Many architects, for example, are under the impression that if an obstruction falls below a line drawn at 45° to the sill of a window, the light of the room served by that window cannot be injured. This ignores completely the layout of the room behind the window, and a simple sectional elevation will soon make this clear (see Figure 9). That the 'rule' sometimes works can be likened to saying that all cats are black, and relying on the fact that quite a few are.

It seems an awful waste to spend so much time in proving a negative, but there have been so many cases where people have gone astray in relying on this so-called rule, that it may be worth reiterating.

The height of the window, too, can be very relevant, as another illustration will show (see Figure 10).

It would be convenient if the tests shown above were all that was necessary. A simple line from the building opposite to the head of the affected window is certainly a much better rough and ready guide than any line from the sill. However, it is by no means enough.

Waldram diagrams

Please note that John's original explanations are largely reproduced below, but relate more particularly to the manual method of calculation, whereas now the work is largely carried out using specialist computer software. Far and away the best method of measuring sky visibility within a room is by using a Waldram diagram. This was 'invented' by Percy J. Waldram and is a method of showing on a flat piece of paper, and from thence on to recognisable floor plans, the curved and three-dimensional effects of the real world. On to his diagram you plot in plan and elevation the outlines of the window you are studying, measured from a suitable point in the room at table height (2 feet 9 inches, or 838.2mm). John correctly pointed out that the

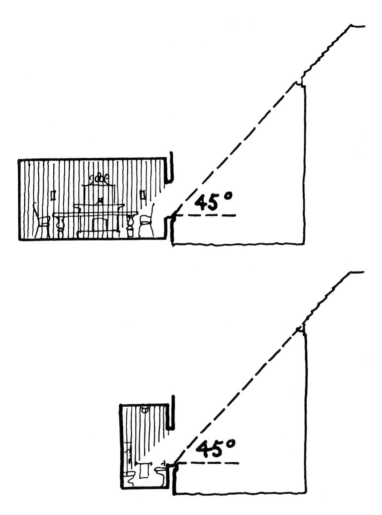

Figure 9: The 45° fallacy: 1
What lies behind a window is very relevant. The same obstruction
will injure a boardroom, but be harmless to a cloakroom

conventional approach is to adopt the unglazed, or
masonry, opening of the window for your calculations,
because glazing bars and the like may change, while the
basic aperture is likely to remain unaltered. However,

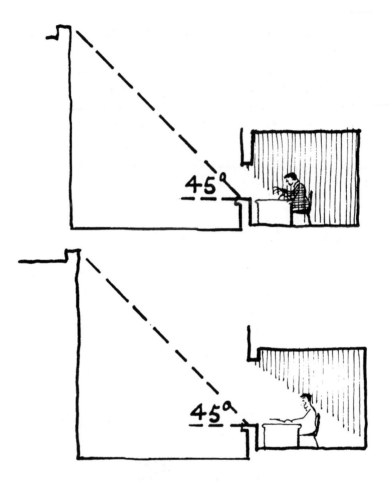

Figure 10: The 45° fallacy: 2
The head height of the window in relation to floor level can
substantially affect light penetration. Sill height is largely irrelevant

Lance had a case two or three years ago where he was
called in to assist someone with a simple residential
extension and the consultant representing the neighbour
queried the Anstey Horne & Co. technical assessment
because it did not take account of numerous glazing bars
– a Georgian type arrangement. In order to try to placate

the surveyor and at the same time organise an amicable settlement, Lance prepared – not himself you understand because he has neither the skill nor the inclination – a computer study based upon the conventional approach and with the glazing bars included in every detail. He was surprised, and had to admit to the other surveyor, that it did make a reasonably significant difference. The reason was partly because the relevant offending structure was set at an angle to the window in question, so that from within the room the glazing bars effectively appeared closer together and obstructed the light to a greater extent than first thought.

From accurate surveys, you plot the existing obstructions to light, not forgetting distant ones which may be relevant, and you produce a curious curved picture in which a patch or patches of sky will be found. These are measured, and can be compared to the whole dome of sky at the same scale – a single Waldram diagram shows half the whole dome (which is itself a hemisphere). If the area of the patches is greater than 0.2% of that whole dome, you pick a point further back in the room and try again. If it is less, then you move forward.

When you have plotted enough points, you can draw a contour of 0.2% sky visibility. The whole exercise is then repeated for the new conditions and a second contour drawn.

Sometimes, the starting point for your 'before' contour will be an agreement. The building you are studying may be the subject of a deed which permits it to be carried up to a certain height, but in fact it is intended to make it higher still. In that case, your 'before' contour is not that which shows the light as it is at present in the dominant

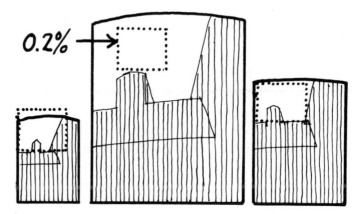

Figure 11: Not too little, not too much, but just right: the patches of sky which may be shown up on your Waldram diagram studies. If you obtained the first image from your chosen point, you should try another one, further forward; if the second, you should move backwards in the room; if the last, cheer and move sideways

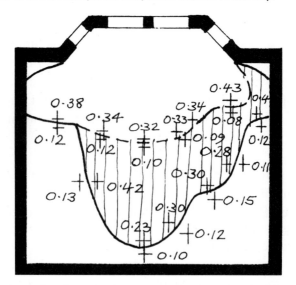

Figure 12: The solid line represents the 0.2% contour in the 'old' conditions; the dashed line shows the 'new'. It may be necessary to study a number of points within a room in order to obtain the two contours, but it is not necessary to find the exact 0.2% points on those lines. You can extrapolate from near misses and still be reasonably accurate

96

premises, but what that light would be if the permitted building were carried out.

Assessing injury

You are now in a position to assess whether any injury has been or will be suffered (or caused). These alternatives matter, because you may be carrying out your assessment on behalf of a dominant owner *or* a servient one, and you may be doing so before the old building is taken down, after the new building has gone up or – the most difficult – when the old building has gone and the new has not yet come.

The experienced rights of light consultant learns to reconstruct, in his mind, buildings that have been demolished, using clues like the remnants of an old flashing, or brickwork which was obviously not intended to be exposed to the weather. The maps produced by Charles E Goad Ltd are very useful in this respect. By finding an edition for the appropriate year, you can often get a very good idea of what buildings were formerly on a now cleared site. Sometimes, indeed, all that needs to be done is to complete a terrace, mentally. The consultant has also to try to create in his mind a new building or a new extension – as high as that sill, and as far out as that tree, for example – or a complete new office block, with a three-storey podium and a ten-storey tower. You will realise that making an on-site estimate of the likely effect of that sort of building is both difficult and dangerous. You can only risk it when you're very experienced and the result is not likely to be critical. Also, this kind of approach is only appropriate when offering preliminary advice.

If you are acting for the dominant owner, looking from inside the may-be-injured window, it is a lot easier to guess and, on the whole, less serious if you get it a little wrong. In the vast majority of cases, however, accurate surveys of the existing conditions, relating the site of the proposed building to the possibly affected windows, are absolutely essential, and must be very accurate indeed for any case which is going to court. The rest of your evidence is not likely to be regarded as reliable if cross-examination shows your plans to be inaccurate.

When you are assessing the situation for a potential developer, however, you can hardly walk in next-door and say: 'we may be going to affect you, so can we have some plans, please'. There you have to rely on much less accurate measurements, and the client has to be told of the limitations. You will probably have to count brick courses and estimate distances, and even that without being observed to be doing so.

John would recall one case where he had to lean out of a window and guess at an effect some hundred feet away or so and round a corner: He guessed at 'a couple of thousand pounds' damage. Later, he was able to get close, and said 'about £10,000'. When he was able to measure it from inside, because a claim had been made, it came to £15,000 – the claim had been for £40,000. The client was not best pleased at this escalation, but John was able to point out that he had always expressed the inaccuracy of the method of assessment he was being forced to use. With hindsight, he always said that he wished he had expressed it more forcefully.

Relevant obstructions

You must be careful to take account of all relevant obstructions. A distant tower block may fill a very critical gap in the skyscape, while a large chimney stack in the old conditions may be enough almost completely to negate the effect of a new storey upon one window, while making no contribution to the effect upon another. Make sure that a photographic record, at least, of your client's old building is taken before it is demolished – while in critical cases, nothing less than a full survey is desirable.

Reliance on photographs

Photographs alone can be very misleading, and a few carefully noted measurements can save hours of poring over confusing photographs. Sometimes, of course, you will have been instructed too late, and will have to rely on what can be found, and may end up staring through

Figure 13: 'Since a crooked figure may attest in little place a million' the relationship of large chimney stacks on the 'old' building to the windows in the dominant tenement can be equivalent almost to an entire storey on the 'new' building

magnifying glasses, until you are dizzy or at old photographs in newspaper offices or libraries, trying desperately to work out what the old obstructions were. If you yourself are taking the photos, try to take them so that they relate to each other, and to an OS map on which you have marked the points from which they were taken. Note also whether they were taken from the roof, ground level, or somewhere in between.

The plant rooms

When considering a proposed building (and old ones too, for that matter) look out for the plant rooms. Architects don't think that they're very important, and they will often be missing from early editions of plans, to be added on at a later stage. They can be critical to rights of light, however, as they very often form the effective skyline to be considered.

Other contours

You may not always be asked simply to measure 0.2% contours. In one case, John acted for tenants whose landlords proposed to substitute tinted glass for clear in their windows. The tenants were concerned that this would mean a substantial reduction in daylight within their offices, and John was asked to calculate the effect. He obtained figures of translucence for the new material from the manufacturers, and then worked out what percentage sky factor would be needed to obtain the same amount of light as clear glass would produce from 0.2% of sky. The loss was then shown by the variation between those two contours.

Agreeing with the opposition

If you do find yourself going to court try, with the approval of your clients and lawyers, to agree your plans with the opposition. If you have made a mistake, it's better to find it out in conversation with your opposite number than in open court, and if *he* has, it may be that you can persuade him that his side ought to withdraw, or at least change their tune.

A lot to do with rights of light is a matter of opinion, especially since *Ough v King*. The actual measurement of sky visibility, however, can be an exact science, so you should use your very best endeavours to see that you carry it out with the utmost precision of which you are capable and which the circumstances allow.

Use of computer programs

Although the Waldram diagram study can be undertaken either manually or by computer, currently the manual method described by John earlier is rarely used and is becoming a dying art. It is an inevitable consequence of the computerised society we live in and if we can calculate matters to umpteen decimal points, why shouldn't we. However, there are unfortunate knock-on effects, as follows. First, a number of would-be rights of light consultants seem to be of the opinion that once they obtain the relevant bit of software they have 'arrived', whereas there is a good deal more to being a good rights of light consultant than being able to produce fancy computer studies. Secondly, there is a tendency to assume that computer studies are accurate because they look nice and pretty. Computers have a mind of their own on occasions and it sometimes takes an experienced eye to spot where the relevant sky factor contours produced by computer simply cannot be correct. Computers therefore have their place, but they are not a substitute for careful and proper consideration by the consultant.

neighbour, and both enjoying all the same benefits except one: the light of one is the new conditions, the light of the other is the old. Would your adversary bid the same by way of capital or rent for the two properties? If he says that he would, you might as well give up talking to him and see him in court. If he honestly replies that he would not, you explain that your valuation exercise is directed at finding out by how much his bid for one should exceed his bid for the other. The answer equals the loss suffered.

The approved method

John explained what he described as 'the approved method' in some detail. This 'approved' method remains intact and in use and his excellent explanations are recited below. However, later in this chapter Lance explores in more detail, an alternative, often more commercial approach, where rather than the starting point being the diminished value of the affected property one seeks to assess the extent to which the developer is gaining at the expense of his neighbour's light.

In the chapter on measurement you learnt how to draw contours of adequacy in old and new conditions. The area over which the contour moves is the area of loss.

Sometimes, owing to a great change in the shape of the servient building, there will be areas of gain as well: it may be appropriate for these to be deducted from the losses. The area of net loss must be very carefully calculated, not a difficult exercise using computer software, but a potentially lengthy process if undertaken manually.

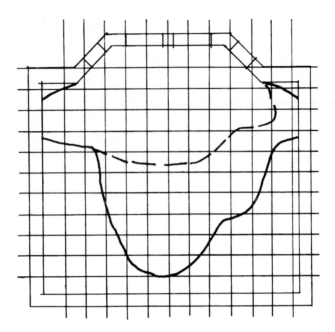

Figure 14: Applying a grid of square feet makes it comparatively simple to measure the loss of well-lit space in the area between the old, solid line and the new, dashed one. (Roughly 37 square feet at a glance. Check it for yourself.)

The grid (see Figure 14) will make it easier for you to check all the necessary measurements: room area and 50% area, together with well-lit areas lost and remaining.

It is also necessary to measure the area of the whole room in order to be able to assess first, whether there has been an injury, and secondly, if there has, how serious it is. You will remember that we have recommended sticking to the 50/50 rule for commercial premises at least: your next task is therefore to measure how much of the room remains within the 0.2% (well-lit) contour. That must then be expressed as a percentage of the whole room area, so that you can decide whether to proceed any further with the valuation. We would repeat that, in commercial cases, if the area still adequately lit is over 50%, you may fairly safely say that there is no injury. If you are dealing with a domestic case, you will be in some doubt between 50% and 55%, but fairly – note, not wholly – confident at over the latter figure.

When you have a whole set of measurements – of the room, the area remaining well lit, and the area of loss – you must then produce a table from them. The table in Figure 15 was the example put forward by John Anstey in the previous edition. It is repeated here, but Lance points out that subtle variations on this method are currently being employed in the rights of light field, and discussion between the leading practitioners may be needed in order to return to a commonly accepted method. For the purposes of this chapter, John's original approach and figures have been used.

You will now see the reason for all the measurements which you have so painstakingly calculated, counted or guessed. The half room area is a fundamental calculation, together with the area remaining well lit, because if the latter is greater than the former, there is no injury in that room, at least if you adopt the 50/50 rule. Don't forget, however, that if one room is actionably injured, other rooms in the same ownership can also come into the loss calculations, even if they would not rank as actionably injured on their own. The second-floor rooms in the table in Figure 15 are two such. They come under the heading of parasitical injuries, about which we shall say a little more near the end of this chapter.

In the next few paragraphs, we will examine another example, where the maths may be easier to follow than in the table of real-life figures.

If you look at Figure 15, the front, first (1st), second (2nd) and makeweight (Mkwt) areas are all part of the net loss area. The 'EFZ' stands for 'equivalent first zone', which is a reduction of the other areas by arithmetical means. The system works like this: let us assume a room area of 200 square feet, an old, well-lit area of 160 square feet, and a new of 30 square feet. One way of expressing that loss would be to say that it was 130 square feet, but in the method adopted by the leading consultants, the area of 130 square feet is broken down into very serious loss, serious loss, fairly important loss, and not very important loss, which correspond to the four headings mentioned at the beginning of this paragraph.

Rights of Light :
Table of Areas (nearest sq. ft.) & Analysis of Loss

FLOOR/ ROOM	WHOLE ROOM	HALF ROOM	PREV. +0·2%	NEW +0·2%	LOSS	Front	1st	2nd	Mkwt	EFZ
6/1	716	358	698	85	613	68	179	366		**464**
6/2	108	54	107	10	97	17	27	53		**79**
1/1	88	44	69	39	30		5	25		**18**
1/2	188	94	96	60	36		34	2		**35**
1/3	389	194	267	111	156		83	73		**120**
2/1	107	53	107	70	37				37	**9**
2/2	24	12	24	20	4				4	**1**
Totals:					**973**	85	328	519	41	**726**

Figure 15: A table of atypically large losses, as produced for working out equivalent first zone areas, from which compensation is eventually calculated

The authors consider that any loss which falls into the area of the room between 50% and 25% well-lit is standard, or first zone loss. In the example we are currently examining, that would be exactly 50 square feet. Any loss between 50% and the rest of the room would not be actionable in itself, but would form part of the loss once an actionable injury had been suffered by the loss creeping over the 50% line – in fact, more than creeping in this example. That injury is therefore reckoned at half value, and a shorthand way of doing the calculation to which we shall eventually come is by halving the area. The 60 square feet of loss is therefore shown in the second zone column, and eventually equals 30. Similarly, in the table, 366 square feet in room G/1 gets added in as 183.

If any loss is serious enough to impinge on the first (or last, depending upon how you look at it) 25% of the room, its importance means that it needs to be multiplied by one and a half, producing, in this case, 30 instead of 20 square feet, and 68 for G/1 equals 102. It is when the front zone figures start to mount up, by the way, that you should be worrying about possible injunctions. Let us be quite clear, while we're on the subject, about 'front' zone. It does not necessarily mean – and is therefore rather a misnomer – the area nearest to the front wall or window of the room. It means the last 25% of well-lit area, which *may* be at the front of the room.

If you had a very small window, giving a narrow shaft of light right to the back of a room, it could be that any obstruction to that window would produce front zone loss – against the back wall. Now let's return to the mathematics.

Adding together the figures we have produced above gives a figure of 110 square feet, expressed in the

60%, SAY, REMAINS TO O·2%S.F.
— NO ACTIONABLE INJURY.
ALL LOSS "MAKEWEIGHT."
✱ N·B. NEARNESS OF LOSS TO
   WINDOW IS IRRELEVANT·

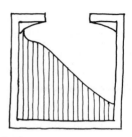

40%, SAY, REMAINS TO O·2%SF.
— ACTIONABLE INJURY
SOME "1st", SOME "2nd "LOSS

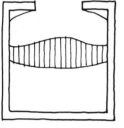

30%, SAY, REMAINS TO O·2%SF.
— ALL LOSS "1st"

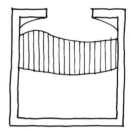

15%, SAY, REMAINS TO O·2%S.F.
— SO SOME "1st", SOME "FRONT
   LOSS·

Figure 16

equivalent of first zone areas: hence, EFZ. When many rooms in one building are affected, some may suffer losses which would not be actionable in themselves, as the room remains well lit: two such are illustrated in Figure 15. Those losses nevertheless have to be taken into account as makeweight, and their areas are divided by four. John always valued staircases and lavatories in commercial buildings as makeweight (and so does Lance). If the contrary is argued, ask whether a tenant expects to pay the full figure per square foot for such areas.

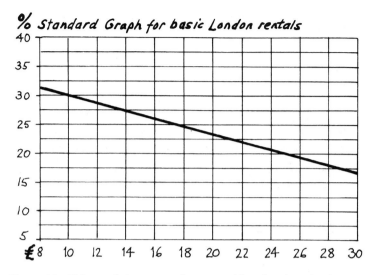

Figure 17: This graph is more or less argued by all today's leading rights of light practitioners as showing the percentage or rack rental value per square foot attributable to natural light

Value of light as a proportion of rent

John referred to the described method of valuation evolving through many meetings and discussion between the leading consultants at the time. They also agreed that the value of light as a proportion of rent varied according to the importance of position and other factors so that, as a general rule, the higher the rent, the lower the percentage attributable to light. A graph was drawn up that enabled consultants to read off a figure for light against any rental figure. John identified the three leading consultants at the time as his father, Bryan Anstey, Keith MacDonald and Eric Arnall. In the early days of John's eminence his contemporary was Eric Roe (now retired) who took over from Keith MacDonald at Wilks Head & Eve. It is probably fair to say that John and Eric Roe ruled the roost in London, with a trio of eminence restored by Michael Pitts from his base in Liverpool. To some extent the combined weight – metaphorically speaking – of John, Eric Roe and Michael Pitts carried that methodology through for many years, relatively unquestioned. That is still true in part today with us current, lesser mortals, but in recent years Lance has sensed increasing unease – perhaps uncertainty is a better word – in the ranks of his fellow consultants on the subject. Nothing has yet changed but this chapter explores, albeit a bit later on, where there are at least question marks as to whether the methodology needs to be revised, or at least applied a little more flexibly in certain circumstances.

The original graph, (Figure 17) prepared by Bryan Anstey, Keith MacDonald and Eric Arnall, effectively had to be revised when, during the 1980s, the extremely high level rents prevailing arguably distorted the light values obtained using the graph. So many other factors were now inflating rents, such as the availability of computer channelling, and big, open dealing floors, that even applying the lowest percentage shown in the original graph produced a figure which John certainly felt clearly exceeded the true value of the daylight.

A new consultants' conference was called, at which the successors of two of the original three were present, and the third's successor was kept informed since he was unable to be there; three of the newcomers to the sport were also present. All agreed that for London rents even in excess of £50 per square foot, no more than £5 should be adequate to represent the value of the light (see Figure 18). No premises were then available at the lowest figure shown on the old graph (at Figure 17), and so a new starting point was chosen. For areas outside London, it

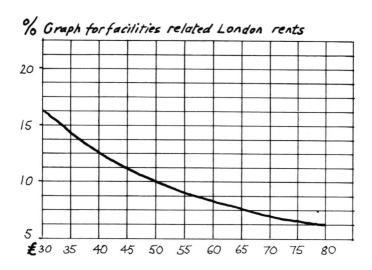

Figure 18: This graph indicates that, however high the rent being paid for 'high tech' facilities, the amount of the rent attributable to light is never more than £5

was agreed that similar principles should be followed, but the wide variation in provincial values, coupled with the narrower range of rents in any one of those centres, made it difficult to settle upon one particular scale or graph, although it was possible to produce a tentative one (see Figure 19).

John explained that the new graphs (Figures 18 and 19) were not 'formally' adopted in the way that (Figure 17) was, but it is pretty certain that something very close to them will be at some point, so we will risk producing them here for your delectation, including one which indicates the light value of £5, whatever the 'high tech' rent.

Once the rental value had been agreed the mechanical steps set out above could be employed to arrive at a base

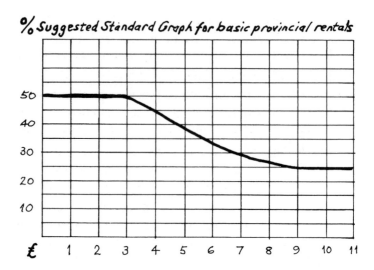

Figure 19: This is a very tentative graph indicating the sort of percentages which might be used to derive the value of light from provincial rents

figure, commonly referred to as the 'book value' of the infringement. John correctly pointed out the need, on occasions, to seek expert valuation advice. He recited the example of cities where he had no first-hand recent knowledge of rentals, but even in London – his base and now Lance's – rental values are extremely variable from location to location and local knowledge is vital. For the same reason, advice is often also welcome on capitalisation, since the last task is to arrive at a capital figure for the injury, which you get by multiplying the light rental value by the EFZ and then by the appropriate YP (years' purchase).

Freeholder in possession

John also correctly asserted that rights of light consultants commence the valuation of injuries on the basis of a freeholder in possession, but also pointed out that there may be several interests in the dominant tenement, all of which have to be appeased, depending upon the terms of their leases and whether the landlord has reserved all rights of light to himself. His conclusion was therefore that the developer may be asked for several cheques, but they should all add up to the number he first thought of – the freeholder in possession number. Lance adds that while this is entirely correct in principle, in practice it is sometimes necessary for the servient tenement to pay more, effectively 'over the odds' to get everyone signed up. The point being that if one is paying compensation one is dealing with an actionable and thereby at least potentially injunctable loss. Therefore, one has to satisfy all interested parties – those with rights in law – in order to be certain of one's position. If one lessee holds out for a larger sum because he is greedy, does not understand the way the law works or simply does understand the relative strength of his position in terms of holding the developer to ransom, the developer may happily pay the larger sum to avoid a confrontation and complete the exercise. Therefore, in theory one should be able to calculate the loss for a freeholder in possession and worry about dividing it up later, but life in the development world does not always work out so easily.

As this is a chapter, not a treatise, on valuation, we are going to have to assume a certain degree of knowledge on the part of you, the readers. If you don't understand the concept of YP, which we are about to employ, you must either read a general book on valuation, or ask someone to explain.

In order to apportion the 'freeholder in possession' sum between the said freeholder, the long leaseholder, and the occupying tenant, you will need a copy of Parry. Using the single rate table in this, with no allowance for tax, and choosing the percentage column appropriate to the YP you have used in capitalising the compensation in the first place, you can read off the multipliers to be used according to the period up to the next rent review.

Let us look at a typical example. You have agreed an injury of 300 square foot EFZ, and a light value of £5, producing an annual figure of £1,500. You then agree a YP of 18 to produce a capital figure of £27,000. There is an occupying tenant with three years to go to his next rent review, and a head lessee with 27 years left without review. The argument is that at a review (for any lessee) the rent will be assessed in the light (joke) of the prevailing circumstances, and so each is only affected until the next review.

Find the column in Parry closest to 18 YP, which is 5.5%, of which the perpetuity figure is actually 18.1818. Divide your capitalised total by 18.18. You may ask why we didn't multiply the £1,500 by 18.1818 in the first place. The answer is because we probably didn't have Parry open at the time, and having agreed upon a figure of 18 YP and its resultant capital product, the paying-out side is not going to be keen to agree a higher figure now just in order to simplify the calculations. Nobody is going to lose by this method, at least not in relation to the capital sum agreed in the first place. So, to repeat, you divide by 18.18 to produce a slightly different annual figure. The answer is £1,485 (or as near as makes no difference). We may have to juggle a pound or two later to make everything fit.

Looking down the 5.5% column to three years, we find a multiplier of 2.6979, which we will call 2.7. That times

£1,485 equals £4,009 and is the occupier's share. Next we find the head lessee's terminal date of 27 years, and a multiplier of 13.8981 which for the sake of simplicity, we will round off to 13.9. You must deduct the 2.7 already paid to the tenant, and then multiply £1,485 by 11.2, producing £16,632. Theoretically, you should now be confident that, as £16,632 plus £4,009 equals £20,641, the sum of £6,359 is the freeholder's share. However, you should always carry out one last calculation to make sure you've done the others correctly – just as we will do here.

We know that the perpetuity figure is 18.18, so we deduct the 13.9 already distributed, leaving 4.28, which, times £1,485, produces £6,356. We've therefore got three pounds to play with from our various simplications, so we'll give one to each party. The tenant gets £4,010, the head lessee £16,633 and the freeholder £6,357.

What is the position if the freeholder has reserved all rights of light matters to himself? One very distinguished authority argues that, as he will suffer no damage until the date of his reversion, he should only get the compensation deferred: the £6,357 in our example above. Others disagree. Theoretically, in John's opinion (he was one of those to disagree), the lessee will have reduced his bid if he is going to have to take the kicks of loss of light without the ha'pence of compensation. The landlord will therefore already be in receipt of less money than if he had allowed the tenant to participate in any prospective loss, and so he is entitled to receive the whole sum (in the example) of £27,000. John would agree that, in fact, this calculation would be unlikely to have been done by the prospective tenant – though it's quite possible that the landlord would have done it – but he felt that the theory was correct.

Agreeing rights of light compensation

As you may by now be rather confused, we will set out again, but very simply (and not in the same order) the steps to agreeing rights of light compensation:

- agree the rent, and then the value of the light in that rent, probably using the 'agreed' graph;
- agree the appropriate YP;
- measure the areas of room, old well-lit, new well-lit, and thence the loss;
- apportion the areas of loss according to degree of seriousness, and reduce them to equivalent first zone (EFZ) in square feet;
- multiply your three factors together: EFZ, rate and YP; and
- if necessary, apportion the capital compensation between the various interests.

Valuation of domestic property

The valuation of domestic property is in many ways more difficult. Values per square foot are not always appropriate or available, so one has to take an empirical view, based on capital values. The value of a particular room has to be considered and staircases, for example, which may be of little value in commercial premises, can be the sole means of communication between important parts of a dwelling, often used in twilight hours, so that daylight is very important indeed – Lance admits to placing less importance upon staircases, even in a dwelling. Lavatories and bathrooms are of slight importance, in daylight terms. You may have some considerable difficulty in agreeing the value of a domestic injury, but let us assume that you eventually do.

Blackmail

Having spent several pages explaining in very clear terms the basic methodology, John previously rounded off this chapter by introducing what he described quite bluntly, but in truth, quite accurately, as 'blackmail'. This edition of the book expands a little upon John's comments, not only because it is quite fun to use provocative terms such as blackmail, but also because the long-established and tried and tested formula is increasingly nothing more than a starting point from which the commercial realities of life kick in.

Blackmail is not a dirty word in rights of light circles. It is, rather, a short and convenient way of describing the fact that, in commercial cases where both parties know perfectly well that the dominant owner could certainly obtain an injunction if he put his mind to it, the servient owner is going to have to pay well over the odds in compensation. The figure can range from about one and a half times the book value to almost any number you care to think of: half of the extent of the development value which could not be achieved without the dominant owner's acquiescence should be regarded as the maximum – and that not frequently attained. When Lance first became actively involved in the rights of light field – regularly acting as a consultant – he believed there seemed to be a sense of immorality or inappropriate behaviour when the dominant tenement sought to extract a sum of compensation more related to their developer neighbour's gain than their loss. Developers still have a tendency to think in those terms but in Lance's opinion he feels that this commercial approach is appropriate in some cases, and has no shame in pursuing such a claim on behalf of a client if the right circumstances prevail.

After all, why should an injured party give up his light and agree not to pursue an injunction that might otherwise be his entitlement, only to receive a moderate sum of compensation and at the same time allow his developer neighbour to make a fortune as a consequence?

Where one is seeking to base a claim on a share of the developer's net gain it is necessary to carry out a valuation exercise that may extend significantly beyond the expertise of the rights of light consultant. The consultant can do the first part, which is to assess the extent to which the proposed development would have to be adjusted to avoid an actionable injury – quite a complicated exercise in itself because as we know the law is not black and white – but is unlikely to have the necessary skills to then calculate the difference in value between the proposed building and the smaller, cutback version that respects rights of light. He may, given the right technology in his office, be able to calculate the reduction in gross floor space, but not the complications that might arise with regard to loss of service cores, devalued space arising out of a resultant inappropriate floor plate, etc.

An additional factor is the almost certain need for the developer to seek a revised planning permission if his proposed scheme already has a consent in place. Once a rights of light consultant has hacked around the massing of the building to respect rights of light, this might well lead to being left with a wholly unbuildable form and shape, requiring even further amendment to make it aesthetically acceptable, suitable in streetscape terms, etc.

You will gather by now that a developer can run into enormous difficulty when causing an injunctable loss of light and any compensation paid to his neighbours, even if he is lucky enough to get to that point, might extend well beyond what in theory his neighbour is losing.

In conclusion, pursuing a claim based upon a share of a developer's gain is no easy matter and can be wholly impractical. It can be a relatively easy exercise where one has a uniform form of development opposite one affected neighbour, such that there are no other parties to get in the way and complicate matters. If, on the other hand, there are half a dozen properties opposite the proposed development, they are all likely to be affected to some extent and bearing in mind that the science of light is a three-dimensional affair, it is highly likely that each of the six properties will be affected by the same element of the new building also affecting their neighbours. In situations such as this a court may find it very difficult to agree upon a fair and reasonable valuation exercise related to development gain.

The approach of the courts

This leads on to the approach of the courts, where ultimately all such matters are settled in the event of dispute. Current case law seems to confirm that the principle of claims made on the basis of a share of development gain is likely to be accepted in the right circumstances, but courts will generally expect there to be some reasonable correlation between the loss suffered by the neighbour and the gain enjoyed by the developer. In other words, if the injury to the neighbouring property were technically actionable, but quite small such that it would give rise to a compensation figure of say £10,000 using the traditional method of valuation, they would be disinclined to go along with a claim for £1m using the development gain principle. They might adopt the view that the sum being sought were too far removed from the neighbour's alleged loss and look towards some form of 'reasonable' compromise.

Lance is often asked what percentage of the developer's net gain a court is likely to award. Obviously, that does depend upon the circumstances of the case, the size of the figures involved, etc., but the general view seems to be that a figure of around a third would not be wholly unrealistic. Lance is not sure how much that relates back to the *Stokes v Cambridge* principle, but it is certainly not a rule of law. One hears on the grapevine of a case where the developer agreed to pay virtually the whole of his development gain to extract himself from a clearly injunctable position, but unaware of the circumstances – obviously quite extreme and probably involving the developer buying himself out of restrictive covenant or some other difficult circumstance – it is impossible to comment in any meaningful way.

The message one must deliver to developer clients is not just that they cannot force the neighbours to accept compensation, but also that there are occasions where compensation claims may extend well beyond a fair and reasonable sum based upon their neighbour's loss.

So now on to a more pleasant subject.

13 Fees

John suggested that if he had charged on a percentage basis throughout his career, he would have lived a life of comfortable affluence, devoting most of his time to writing books on abbeys, castles and Venice, while doing the odd consultancy of national importance just to keep his hand in. However, his view was that if he had done so he would have then been vastly overpaid for the amount of work he actually had to carry out. Was he right? On balance Lance considers his view was correct and it is fair to say that today the leading consultants almost exclusively charge on an hourly rate basis, but there are occasions when the fee may reflect what is recorded on a time sheet, but does not perhaps fully reflect the expertise of the consultant and the resultant advantage – normally some form of financial gain – for the client.

In Lance's entire career to date he has not yet charged on a percentage or any other type of incentive based arrangement and has rarely felt aggrieved on the subject. However, he recalls an out-of-London project for a major property company, where it had been approached by a neighbouring developer with an offer to pay compensation and needed advice as to the strength of its position. The company had not fully appreciated the strength of its position and on the back of Lance's advice managed to extract somewhere in the region of £2m, despite the fact that it was generally supportive of the development proposal and keen to see it proceed – general uplift in the area, the setting of a precedent for tall buildings, etc. Lance was delighted to know the outcome of his advice and when invited to submit a fee account he reported that while his time sheets recorded something equating to a nominal fee of around £1,500, that did not seem to fairly represent the value of his advice. Lance therefore suggested that they advise him as to what they considered it reasonable to pay; the grateful client responded promptly suggesting that he forward an account in the sum of £1,500! This perhaps ties in with John's analogy of the surgeon who was asked to itemise his bill of 100 guineas for an appendectomy. He replied: 'to taking out appendix, £5; to knowing how to take out appendix, £100'.

Why not fixed fee?

Most clients would prefer that rights of light consultants worked on the basis of fixed fees and one can understand why, but rarely is it a practical solution. The reason is quite simple, at the outset rarely does anyone know how much work is going to be required of the consultant. Lance is happy to quote a fixed fee when first instructed, to visit site, consider the position and to submit a preliminary report. However, from that point on it all becomes very much more difficult to predict.

One of the obvious difficulties is predicting what the reaction of affected neighbours will be. If they happen to be greatly offended by the proposal, turning into vociferous planning objectors and litigants, the consultant may have a large and important part to play in the project. If, on the other hand, the neighbours are relatively relaxed, perhaps not even understanding their rights and strength of their position, little or no problems may arise. Perhaps it is fair to say that most clients understand and respect the consultant's position, but it still leaves them uncomfortable initially.

Another problem, to some extent a more recent phenomenon, is the need to carry out detailed technical studies for either common law or planning purposes, very often both. Presumably, in years gone by, leading consultants visited site, made an estimation and based their advice on not much more, reserving formal technical studies – then carried out manually – for the more complicated and sensitive cases. Times have changed, the world is a more litigious place and generally there is a greater awareness of the subject of rights of light. Developers and their funders are therefore keener than ever to establish their position and risk with greater certainty, as a consequence of which detailed technical studies are now the norm on virtually any sizeable project and it is not simply a question of analysing what the client or architect has in mind. That may be the starting point and if one is lucky it could be the finish as well, but more often than not it is necessary to work closely with the architect and client to work up a revised form of massing that provides a safer position with regard to both the common law and planning elements. That can involve looking at various different options, particularly on larger schemes, and there is simply no way of predicting the level of technical input required at the outset.

The problem is eased where the consultant works regularly with a particular client because there is a greater degree of understanding and, very importantly, trust.

Lance is confident that some of his better clients could not tell you what his current hourly rate is, but he would like to think they are confident that he will do the job they require and charge them a reasonable fee at the end of the day.

Lance believes that it is not his place to advise as to what is an appropriate hourly rate is for a leading rights of light consultant and on hourly rates he would simply leave you with John's approach: 'I should point out that I reckon I am the best there is, and that nobody else should be charging more than me – if I find out that they are, I put my charges up'. Typical John Anstey, but probably justifiable arrogance.

Assistants

As to assistants' time, as in every other professional discipline it will depend on the level of experience of the individuals involved. It is possible to utilise building surveying assistants for certain elements of a consultant's work, but do not let them loose on the more complex issues, including report writing and letters providing formal advice to clients. It is a very dangerous approach and you will receive no sympathy from your clients or insurers.

It tends to be the case that clients do not expect to pay high hourly rates for technical assistants, yet Lance's own technical team play a vital part in allowing him to function properly and efficiently. He therefore pays them what they are worth to him as opposed to reflecting the hourly rate chargeable for their work as set against other disciplines. Good technical backup is vital to a rights of light consultant, especially now that formal technical studies are the norm rather than the exception to the norm.

Travelling expenses

John made the point that one has to be careful regarding travelling time when visiting a distant site. In that respect Lance does have some sympathy with clients, but the problem arises simply because almost every leading consultant is based in London and rights of light problems can occur anywhere. Lance gets around the problem by keeping his fixed fee for an initial inspection and report almost identical for jobs outside of London, buying a first-class ticket when travelling by train and utilising the travel time to work on other matters.

Another vitally important factor is the proximity of the site to something else of interest! John would travel and charge very moderate fees if it were in a part of the country where there were an interesting abbey or friend to visit. Lance, on the other hand, is more tempted by the best of our fishing rivers, but like John he is honest enough to tell clients the truth so that they can come up with the best possible arrangements for all involved.

Court proceedings

Sitting through court or enquiry proceedings is exceedingly unproductive and can create havoc with one's diary. However, there are occasions where attendance over a period of days is inevitable and that is where one needs good backup from one's team. Lance does not change his own hourly rate for different work items. Nor, does he vary his hourly rate from client to client or depending upon whether he is acting for the developer or the consultant. He abhors the practice of those who will charge a certain hourly rate – a lower figure – to secure work with a regular client, yet will seek an increased rate when acting for an injured party and there is less control over their fee as part of an overall settlement.

Daylight and sunlight: Town and Country Planning

The old Chapter 14 in the third edition of this book was entitled simply 'Planning: personal and public'. Among other things, this chapter provided a brief introduction to the daylight and sunlight issues arising out of the Town and Country Planning process. Since that edition of the book, the position in terms of planning has changed significantly. As briefly referred to in the Introduction to this edition, the question of light in the planning sense now forms a much more significant part of any consultant's workload. Indeed, if there is such a thing as a growth industry in this field, it is that of the daylight and sunlight consultant in respect of the Town and Country Planning process.

Wrongly or rightly, planning authorities are becoming increasingly conscious of the need to protect the environment in general, and neighbouring residential properties in particular. Daylight and sunlight reports based on the 1991 BRE report, 'Site Layout Planning for Daylight and Sunlight: A Guide to Good Practice', in support of planning applications, are now the order of the day, and consultants such as Lance have quickly had to familiarise themselves with the whole planning process to a much more significant extent.

129

An extensive introductory guide to the BRE document wouldn't be entirely out of place at this point. But bearing in mind the rest of the book's concentration on the common law element of rights to light, to do so would affect the balance of the text unacceptably. Readers will therefore have to make do with a preliminary introduction only, and should of course feel free to contact Lance at Anstey Horne & Co if they or their clients require more detailed advice on the subject.

Before we move onto that preliminary introduction, let's look briefly at the key differences between rights of light and daylight and sunlight.

The key differences between rights of light and daylight and sunlight

Though less so than in previous years, Lance still comes across a number of people in the building industry – including those who really should know better – who do not understand the clear distinction between common law and planning issues, and go on to purchase sites on the erroneous basis that with the benefit of planning permission they are free to build out their proposed scheme. How wrong they are.

Rights of light, the common law element, deals with the private rights of one party over another party's land; any dispute between the parties would, ultimately, be settled by the courts if an amicable solution could not be found. As advised earlier in Chapter 10, the court would be in a position to use its discretionary powers and award damages rather than an injunction, if it felt the circumstances were appropriate. These legal rights prevail irrespective of whether the proposed building works have the benefit of planning permission.

Local planning authorities should not – and very rarely do – take account of the legal rights of the parties (the applicant and any objectors), with their task simply being to ensure that local and government planning policy is properly applied and implemented. As part of that process, the impact upon daylight and sunlight to neighbouring properties, and on sunlight to private and public amenity spaces surrounding the site, are properly and fairly protected against an unreasonably adverse impact.

(This issue is unfortunately confused by the fact that the BRE Guide includes a section (Appendix E) specifically related to rights of light and, more importantly, contains a key flow chart dealing with the impact upon daylight to neighbouring properties which commences with the question 'Are rights to light infringed?', the conclusion being that if the answer is 'yes', 'daylighting is likely to be seriously affected'. And thus we have a recipe for confusion and potential dispute. But let's leave that for now.)

Planning officers are not trained in the field of common law rights of light, and it is therefore both unreasonable and wholly impractical to expect them to consider legal niceties, including the potential existence and relevance of rights of light deeds, or similar agreements. They are not capable of taking on that burden, and Lance suspects that any planning authority attempting to dip their toes into rights of light waters would quickly face litigation and cries of improper behaviour.

To conclude, Lance would suggest that readers forget all about common law rights when considering planning applications and any potential daylight and sunlight issues arising therefrom.

The BRE guide: an introduction

Although the BRE guide was first published in 1991 and
to some extent is therefore arguably out of step with
current planning policies, it is the most up-to-date
document available on the subject and, not unreasonably,
is deeply ingrained in the unitary development plans
(UDPs) of most, if not all, local planning authorities in
and around central London. The same probably should
apply once one moves further afield, but it does seem to
be the case that planning authorities in other major cities
are less conscious of the document and its potential
application, with that trend continuing and magnifying as
one moves outwards from any city centre into suburban
locations.

As a consequence of the guide's UDP prominence,
planning authorities tend to apply the guidelines in a
fairly rigid form, looking for 'compliance' in the same
way that they seek adherence to policy in respect of other
relevant planning considerations. Unfortunately, there are
inherent dangers in that approach, because every site is
different, and the rigid application of any one set of
guidelines for every site and location will not always
provide a satisfactory and sensible solution.

For those that suffer the consequences of this approach –
mostly the person desirous of carrying out the building
work, but really anyone involved in the process – the
tendency is to conclude that the guide itself is to blame.
But while it is not a flawless document, in its
introduction section the author, Professor P. J. Littlefair,
clearly sets the scene for use and application of the guide,
noting the following:

'the advice given here is not mandatory and this document should not be seen as an instrument of planning policy ... its aim is to help rather than constrain the designer. Although it gives numerical guidelines, these should be interpreted flexibly because natural lighting is only one of many factors in site layout design ... in special circumstances the developer or planning authority may wish to use different target values.'

The Professor recognises the difficulty – no, impossibility – of coming up with a set of rules that can readily and sensibly be applied in each and every case. He therefore knowingly presents guidelines that provide a useful working basis for planning authorities and designers alike, but which should not be rigidly applied in all instances.

It could well be argued that the guide is out of step and to some extent in conflict with the aims and objectives of planning policy guidance such as PPG3 ('Housing'). It promotes increased densities in urban areas and making the best use of previously developed land in order to improve and increase the existing housing stock. The policy itself may be enlightened, but as a consequence of increased densities, buildings will almost inevitably be taller and sited in closer proximity to one another, such that once again rigid application of the BRE guidelines is not a realistic target. Of course, in some established residential areas and in more suburban locations, a different and more rigid approach may well be justifiable.

Key elements of the BRE guide

In the first few years after the guide was introduced, it was Lance's personal experience that the focus of local planning authorities was on that part of the guide dealing with the impact upon neighbouring properties. That is still a key feature, perhaps still the most important factor, but the guide also includes a significant section dealing with the quality of light within new developments, and it is that part which has come more to the fore in recent times.

This may be partly due to heightened awareness of the need to design new buildings with the quality of the built environment at the forefront of the designer's mind, but it also seems to be a direct consequence of the move towards increased densities in urban environments. Local planning authorities are increasingly being presented with proposals that involve multiple blocks of significant height, with relatively limited amenity spaces between and surrounding them. As a consequence, not only is it necessary to consider the impact upon neighbours, but also whether the new units being provided will enjoy good daylight and sunlight conditions.

Again, it is Lance's opinion that rigid application of the BRE guidelines in this respect is unrealistic in most urban environments, where one expects a denser grain and where surely there cannot be the same expectation of light as in a suburban context. Relaxed targets for certain locations may therefore be appropriate, but that is not always readily accepted by planning officers.

In fairness, the BRE guide does include an appendix section dealing with the setting of alternative target values for skylight access, but it is not terribly easy to apply in practice. Most consultants, developers and planning authorities appear to appreciate the need for additional BRE guidance on how one might apply different target values and tests to cater for urban environments in particular. Lance has gone so far as to suggest to Professor Littlefair that a supplementary guide might be appropriate, to deal with that particular point, as well as to reflect the inevitable changes that have arisen in the years since the guide was first published.

The key tests

It is neither necessary nor practical for this book to explain the technicalities of the relevant tests, but they are listed below in simple form.

The first daylight test

The first daylight test is to take a point at the centre of the lowest affected windows (often at ground floor level, but not always) and to draw a line at 25° from the horizontal. Should any part of the proposed development breach the aforementioned 25° line, there is the potential for a material impact upon daylight and it is recommended that more detailed checks are undertaken. As you can imagine, in urban areas this test is of limited use or relevance.

The VSC test

The first of the detailed tests in this section of the guide is that of vertical sky component (VSC), a measurement of the total amount of skylight available at the centre of each main window, with the reference point being the external plane of the window wall. In Lance's opinion, this test can be misleading in isolation, because it can take no account of the size of the window, the size of the room it lights or the fact that any particular room may be lit by more than one window. However, it is a way of assessing the maximum amount of daylight potential available at the station point chosen.

A VSC target of 27% is set (the maximum being 40% for an unobstructed wall) and the recommendation is that if this target value cannot be met – often the case in built-up urban environments in the existing condition – then the existing VSC value should not be reduced to less than 0.8 times its original value. The inference, rightly or wrongly, is that a reduction in the existing VSC value of less than 20% is not material and will not have an unacceptably adverse impact upon daylight conditions. Some of you might be upset by losing 19% of the daylight to your main reception room.

The Daylight Distribution test

The second detailed test is that of Daylight Distribution, where the distribution of light within the affected room is assessed. There are similarities between this and the type of analysis one undertakes for common law studies, but one of the key differences is that in common law one is testing where an adequate amount of light will penetrate to (the 0.2% standard), whereas this test simply assesses the maximum point of daylight penetration. It may therefore show penetration of daylight to quite a significant depth, even though this may only be through relatively narrow 'slots' between buildings and not provide good quality daylight conditions.

Unfortunately, the guide does not suggest a target as to what area of a room should receive some daylight, simply recommending that the existing day-lit area not be reduced to less than 0.8 times its original value. It could

therefore be that a room receiving some daylight over
something approaching 80% of its total area would fall
foul of strict application of this particular test, when in
fact that level of daylight penetration to rooms on the
lower floors of a building in an urban setting might well
be perfectly acceptable and at or above the norm for the
location.

The ADF test

The third detailed test is that of average daylight factor
(ADF), and is, in a sense, the most comprehensive test.
Not only does it take account of window size, room size
and the possibility of a room being lit by multiple
windows, but also considers additional factors, such as
internal finishes and light reflectance. However, it does
not appear in that part of the guide dealing with testing
the impact upon neighbouring properties, instead being
introduced in the section dealing with quality of light
within new buildings (with the relevant methodology and
targets set out in Appendix C, 'Interior Daylighting
Recommendations').

This test is a point of much debate in daylight and
sunlight circles. For his part, Lance has tended to take a
stand against many fellow consultants who commonly
apply the ADF test when submitting reports to planning
authorities in support of planning applications and when
assessing the impact upon neighbouring properties
(usually limited to those in residential use). While he
recognises the merits of the ADF test in the sense that it
introduces greater detail than the VSC or Daylight
Distribution tests in isolation, the author of the BRE
Guide confirmed to him in writing that it was never
intended to be a test of the impact upon neighbouring

properties. He considers it more appropriate as a design tool – hence its application to the design of light within new developments and its relationship to the British Standard for daylighting and the CIBSE *Applications Manual: Window Design,* which contain advice and guidance on interior daylighting. Professor Littlefair further made the point to Lance that the ADF test is best suited to a situation where the light conditions within a building or a particular room are being assessed by a designer – usually the architect – and where flexibility is available in terms of window dimensions and the like.

Lance would conclude that his approach is technically correct in terms of careful reading and application of the guide, and is also in keeping with the intention of the author. He does not therefore believe that some of his colleagues are correct in applying the ADF test instead of the VSC or Daylight Distribution test, but does concede that there are often occasions where it is a worthwhile test to undertake as a supplementary exercise.

He would add that cynic that he is, he believes that the ADF test is often used in preference to the others because it provides more satisfactory results compared with those arising out of the other tests. However, to be scrupulously fair to those consultants adopting such an approach, he thinks that they would also argue, not entirely unreasonably, that perhaps their clients' proposal should be considered acceptable if it can be proven by means of the ADF test that the affected neighbours would retain a level of daylight generally considered acceptable in the design of new buildings.

Having maintained a consistent approach on this issue over very many projects and several planning appeals and public enquiries where he provided expert evidence, Lance was recently faced with a difficult decision in respect of a planning appeal on a central London site. The appeal team, lead by the applicant's solicitors and barrister, challenged his initial reports because he had 'failed' to include the ADF test, when such results might be favourable from the client's point of view. Despite explaining his rationale in detail, he was requested to carry out an ADF analysis, and when the results turned out to be quite encouraging, was again challenged as to why he was not proposing to include them in his evidence. Although not yielding easily to such pressure, in a desire to avoid being thought obstructive or unreasonable, he agreed to include the ADF results, on the condition that his expert report would clearly explain that it was no more than an additional test in support of his findings in connection with the key designated tests of VSC and Daylight Distribution.

Content with this approach, he proceeded to the appeal, and was immediately attacked in cross-examination for employing a test taken from the wrong part of the guide and which was, therefore, allegedly, wholly inappropriate and inapplicable! Despite his detailed explanations and clear notes in the text of his report explaining the standing and relevance of the ADF test, he was grilled on the subject for some time and accused of applying the guidelines incorrectly. One never expects barristers to play fair in cross-examination, and Lance remains content that his approach was both fair and reasonable, but he may take a little convincing that the ADF test in this context should form a significant part of any future evidence he gives on the subject. This is, he would predict, a debate that will reign for some time.

Sunlight on the face of a building

In terms of sunlight on the face of a building, much like the VSC test, the station point is the centre of the affected window, although this time on the plane of the inside surface of the wall. The test is of what is known as Annual Probable Sunlight Hours, where both summer and winter sunlight levels are assessed. The recommendation in the guide is that if an initial target (again perhaps unrealistic in urban environments) cannot be obtained, the aim should be to avoid reducing existing values to less than 0.8 times their former value. The same point arises as to whether a reduction in sunlight just below 20% should be considered material or not.

Overshadowing of amenity spaces

With regard to the overshadowing of private and public amenity spaces, the guide contains a preliminary area-based test, with the recommendation that one should seek to avoid a situation where a garden or amenity space will be in permanent shadow on 21 March over more than 40% (and preferably no more than 25%) of its total area. If this initial target cannot be met, the recommendation is that the area which can receive some sun on 21 March should not be less than 0.8 times its former value.

Because short glimmers of sunlight can be sufficient to defeat the test of permanent shadow, it is rare, in Lance's experience, that this test is not passed with flying colours. However, the guide itself recognises that this is suitable for no more than a simple, preliminary, assessment and that for critical areas a more detailed study should be carried out.

It is Anstey Horne's practice to pick three or four key dates in the year (perhaps one per season) and to provide overshadowing diagrams for a site and its surrounds at two- or three-hourly intervals. That is a more practical approach and more truly indicative of the overshadowing created by a proposed development.

Quality of light within new developments

Note that when dealing with the quality of light within new developments, clearly it is not a comparison between existing and proposed conditions. For daylight, the VSC and ADF tests are recommended, but in this context the ADF test is more detailed and usually favoured. In terms of sunlight, Annual Probable Sunlight Hours is still the key test, and overshadowing can again be looked at on the basis of a simple area-based test initially, with a more detailed study if required.

The BRE guide is not limited to the tests set out above, but they are perhaps the most important and the most commonly relied upon by all those who work in the field.

Conclusion

The BRE guide is an easy target for developers, consultants and, to some extent planning authorities, but Lance recognises that Professor Littlefair was faced with the impossible task of trying to provide a guide applicable to and suitable for all locations. Having now used it for a number of years, Lance's conclusion is that it is a very useful working guide – a starting point – but should not be applied religiously in each and every circumstance. He also firmly believes that in order to assist with the difficult problem of dealing with daylight and sunlight in an urban environment, and, at the same time, to ensure that the guide is in tune with current policies at local and government level, there is scope for a revised edition of the BRE document. He would welcome the opportunity to offer a consultant's insight to Professor Littlefair in any further research he should undertake.

How to be a rights of light consultant

In the preceding chapters we have tried to give you the background of law and practice that you need to learn in order to be able to advise people about their rights in light matters, whether vis à vis the local council or their neighbours. In the Appendix which follows (to knowing how to write Appendix, £?) we set out a number of leading cases, a thorough knowledge of which will enable you to sound very impressive indeed. But study of this book will not in itself make you an expert – or even a plain old consultant. So what else do you need to set up your plate?

A long apprenticeship may well be the best training, but is not necessarily available to all. If you can't find such an opening, go very gently on your own at first, until you're sure that you can cope with the more complicated sort of jobs. The difficulty inherent in this area is that not only do you have to remember all the law and all the little quirky decisions, some of which we have told you about already, but you also have to be able to make an assessment of the facts of the situation – whether there will be a loss and if so how great – and then put those two or three things together to advise on the best course to pursue.

In the last edition of this book John was keen, and was quite right, to point out the importance of learning how to produce Waldram diagrams, count brick courses, etc. The latter can still be extremely useful, but with the increasing availability of computer software for carrying out rights of light calculation it is fair to say that things have moved on and although learning to carry out Waldram diagrams is still an extremely useful introduction to the subject, it is not the vital ingredient it once was. Lance, after all, was never any good at producing Waldram diagrams and nowadays would not know where to start with one.

Do look for agreements. Ask the client, the solicitors and the architects if they know of any; and then ask again. Look at the buildings involved to decide how old they are. Ask the local authority, both rating and building control departments. Seek out any alterations, and look closely. On one of the very first jobs which John's father allowed John to tackle alone, he was thoroughly deceived by a window which had been moved complete with its surround, and so carefully married to the brickwork around it that he was convinced that it was coeval with the 19th-century building which housed it. (Fortunately, his opponents had made an even more drastic mistake in their proceedings, and a grateful client took him out to supper, which as he noted, doesn't happen too often.)

Don't, unless it's absolutely necessary, and then only with lengthy caveats, try to assess a rights of light situation on the basis of other people's drawings and photographs. They may have failed to draw or photograph the very item – a distant building, an alternative source of light – which swings the whole case.

Don't let clients rush you into an opinion. Often they will go round the building with you and demand to know ('We're exchanging contracts tomorrow') whether there's any risk of an injunction. There's only one answer to that question if they want it quickly: 'Yes'. You need to think carefully about the size of the injury and the nature of the dominant property before you can answer, and the evidence needs time to mature in your head.

Do try to be positive in your advice. Of course you must make it clear when you cannot give an absolutely certain reply. As has hopefully become clear in the course of reading this book, you can never be sure about injunctions, and sometimes not even about whether an injury is actionable, let alone nice points of law. However, as far as is consistent with those uncertainties, be as clear and straightforward as you can in your advice, and don't render it useless with a whole bunch of ifs and buts.

But don't be afraid to give clients the answer they don't want to hear. If someone wants to be told that their light is injured, and you bow to their pressure, you may be allowing them to embark on costly litigation from which, in fact, it is your duty to deter them. They'll blame you quickly enough after losing in court.

Be consistent. Don't argue one way for a developer and another way for a claimant. Be sure your sins will find you out.

Do hedge your opinion with the necessary legal qualifications, but don't be afraid, when necessary, to advise your client to disregard the hedge – like Peter the Great.

Don't attempt to run before you can walk, and don't even walk when you're still a crawler. John was once instructed in a negligence case against a surveyor who, when asked specifically if he was able to deal with rights of light, replied with a categorical affirmative. He wasn't – as he later found out.

And on that subject, do be aware of the dangers from a professional standpoint of taking on rights of light instruction when not sufficiently experienced to do so – in terms of professional indemnity issues and so on.

But, if you can't give advice without looking over your shoulder for a possible negligence claim, don't take the job. John used always to imagine that he carried no insurance, so that he had to make absolutely sure that the advice he gave was correct. He would then imagine (which was of course true), that he was insured to the hilt against any disaster, so that he could give his advice boldly and without fear of any adverse consequences to himself.

Now that you've assimilated all the wisdom offered in the earlier chapters, and taken in all the dos and don'ts of this one, there is only one thing left to do. Read the last chapter and Appendix to put the final polish on your learning, and then go out and be a better consultant than either of these authors. If possible.

Human Rights Act 1998

The *Human Rights Act* 1998 (the 1998 Act) was introduced in 2000 and is potentially relevant to rights of light by virtue of two different sections. Article 1 of the First Protocol deals with 'protection of property' and Article 8 of the Convention deals with rights to protect 'private and family life and home'.

When the 1998 Act first came into force, there was much debate in rights of light circles as to how it would impact upon the question of Crown immunity under section 3 of the *Prescription Act* 1832 (the 1832 Act), and although a slightly clearer picture is starting to emerge, uncertainty still remains. Previously, it was well established that by virtue of section 3 of the 1832 Act, it was not possible to acquire a right to light by prescription (long user) over Crown land. However, that is now in doubt – considerable doubt in fact – and there are potentially significant ramifications for the Crown, other parties with an interest in Crown land and those with an interest in properties adjoining or neighbouring Crown land. Let us consider who is affected and in what way.

The obvious starting point is with the Crown itself, and it is important to remember that the Crown umbrella covers a significant number of parties including, just by way of example, police stations and government offices. If the Crown maintained its *Prescription Act* immunity, it would be free to redevelop and extend on its land without fear of restraint on the basis of a rights of light infringement, albeit still subject to the Town and Country Planning process. In effect, Crown land was therefore rendered more valuable in terms of its development potential and that is where the 1998 Act comes into play because it is, at the very least, questionable as to whether the Crown should enjoy that benefit at the expense of the owners and occupiers of neighbouring properties.

At the time of going to print, Lance was not aware of a decided case establishing that Crown immunity no longer applies by virtue of the provisions of the 1998 Act, but he has had personal experience of projects where the Crown has not seen fit to pursue the question of immunity, despite threatening to do so on one or two occasions.

In one case, which shall of course remain nameless, Lance was acting for the injured neighbour in respect of a large central London development where the freehold was Crown owned, but the development was being undertaken on some form of joint venture basis with a private residential developer. The injury to his client's building was clearly actionable and potentially injunctable, and even though his client was willing to consider settling for a compensation payment, Lance's valuation of the injury was somewhat adrift from that of the developer's consultant. The bullying tactic used by the developers was to employ their solicitors to write to Lance in aggressive terms making it quite clear that they had the benefit of Crown immunity and were simply being 'nice guys' in agreeing to pay a reasonable sum of compensation. Therefore, if Lance did not shut up and take the smaller sum put forward by their consultant, they would utilise section 3 of the 1832 Act and Lance's client would get nothing. Lance was not convinced this was the action of nice guys and with the approval of his client, effectively called their bluff. In order to be in keeping with the tone of the solicitors letters to him, Lance suggested that if they really felt they enjoyed Crown immunity they should get on and use it rather than wasting time threatening it. A dangerous tactic perhaps, but it worked and the nice guys agreed to pay the larger sum that was considered appropriate – Lance leaves it for you to decide whether they were purely trying to be fair and reasonable or were worried about the implications of trying to hide behind the Crown immunity argument.

More recently Lance was involved in a case where he was appointed to advise the developers (headlessees) of a Crown-owned site. Owing to the size of his client's development and the potential impact upon one or two neighbours, he suggested that his clients explore the question of utilising Crown immunity. It was in the interests of the Crown as freeholders to see the development proceed, yet the Crown's solicitors indicated that they did not consider it appropriate to rely upon Crown immunity. They did not see fit to go into detail either, but it certainly appears as though the Crown is becoming increasingly nervous of forcing the issue.

Lance's conclusion, based upon a best guess, is that the Crown has taken detailed legal advice on the subject and while perhaps not willing to concede the point yet, is unlikely to pursue the question of Crown immunity unless forced to do so because it becomes of extreme importance on a particular site. That could lead to a test case and then we will really know where we all stand.

Following on from this, where do potential developers of Crown land stand? The answer must be this: if it transpires that Crown immunity still prevails, they are in a privileged position, making their interest in the Crown property potentially more desirable; if, on the other hand, Crown immunity falls upon the 1998 Act sword, they are back to being in the same position as any other lessee.

In effect, the same points apply, albeit in reverse, with regard to parties that hold an interest in properties overlooking Crown land. If Crown immunity applies they have no recourse if their light is injured, whereas without Crown immunity standing in their way they may be entitled to obtain an injunction or compensation, depending upon the circumstances, in the usual way.

Lance recalls from reading *Rights of Light, the Modern Law* that the authors thought it possible that a Local Authority could suffer at the hands of the 1998 Act because its intention to build and obstruct the light to a neighbouring property might run contrary to section 6 of the 1998 Act, which makes it unlawful for a public authority to act in a way which is incompatible with Convention rights. From a personal perspective Lance has not had any experience of that particular argument being run, but it seems slightly odd to him that a local authority should be constrained to a greater extent than a private individual when the works carried out by a local authority should, in theory at least, be for the greater good. Lance will be looking out for a suitable case on the subject.

Appendix
Some interesting cases

Rights of light law depends heavily upon leading cases, and the discussion of many points during the course of this book has therefore been larded with reference to such cases. It may, however, be helpful as well as interesting for the reader to know a little more about some of the more important cases, including those in which the authors have had some personal involvement. You don't have to read this section if you find it boring: most of the legal principles which arise from these cases should have been incorporated in the text you've already got through.

And of course, the authors would warn you that even leading cases cannot be entirely trusted.

Dent v Auction Mart Company (1866)

Messrs Dents' building stood on the corner of Kings Arms Yard and Tokenhouse Yard, and the Auction Mart Company had bought properties further south in Tokenhouse Yard, which they were proposing greatly to enlarge.

According to one of the plaintiffs' witnesses, the result would be 'to place the staircase windows … in a dismal stagnant well', among other dire effects. The defendants admitted that there would be some effect, but said that it would be very limited, and that they were quite willing to minimise it by using white enamelled tiles.

Some heavy forces were mustered for the battle. There were actually three plaintiffs, who all had one QC in common, but the Attorney-General appeared as leading Counsel for Dent & Co, who took the lead, and the junior was a Mr Kekewich (presumably the one who later became a judge). The case was heard by Sir W. Page-Wood, V-C, who took as his basis for the law to be applied, the words of Best, CJ in *Back v Stacey*, 1826, where he said:

> 'In order to give a right of action and sustain the issue, there must be a substantial privation of light sufficient to render the occupation of the house uncomfortable, and to prevent the plaintiff from carrying on his accustomed business on the premises as beneficially as he had formerly done.'

The Vice-Chancellor proposed substituting 'or' for 'and' in the middle of that quotation, but otherwise completely accepted it.

An ingenious interpretation of beneficial carrying-on of business had been put forward by the defence: that if you did not lose a customer or client, you had suffered no loss. This novelty was rejected by the court. It was also argued that because Dents had said that they would take £2,000 to shut up and go away – an astronomical figure at the time – they had given up their claim to an injunction. John often advanced this line of argument himself, likening the situation to the case of George Bernard Shaw and the actress. He asked her if she would sleep with him for £10,000, and received a favourable response. He then offered £10 and was haughtily asked: 'Sir, what do you think I am, a prostitute?', 'I thought we had settled that question' replied G. B. S., 'and were now only haggling about the price'. However, the court's view in *Dent* was that a figure absurdly over the top really meant that money was not an adequate remedy. Page-Wood reiterated that a neighbour should not be forced unwillingly to take compensation if he preferred to maintain his rights.

In his judgment, the Vice-Chancellor disposed of a great number of arguments that had been put up by the defence. They had wanted less consideration for town houses than country ones; he felt that the law was the same, even if country windows were less likely to be obstructed. They argued that other people made do with less light; he held that the plaintiffs' easement did not entitle them only to other people's bare minimum. The Auction Mart Co said that Dents should have enlarged their windows; Page-Wood answered that it was not for the defendants to tell the plaintiffs how they were to construct their house. Another of the plaintiffs had used Venetian blinds; the judge said that the occasional closing off of light does not mean that the dominant owners should be permanently deprived of it.

Finally, he came to the matter which made this case a particular favourite of John's:

> 'Then, lastly, there was the suggestion of glazed tiles – often made and never listened to by the Court. A person who wishes to preserve his light has no power to compel his neighbour to preserve the tiles, or a mirror which might be better, or to

keep them clean ...; and, therefore, it is quite preposterous to say, "let us damage you, provided we apply such and such a remedy".'

The defendants' QC had urged appointing a jury to view the scene of the crime, but Page-Wood thought that:

'the benefit of a view ... is a good deal exaggerated. If the jury could have had an opportunity of viewing the premises as they existed a year ago, and could be taken to view them as they exist now, the view might be very serviceable. But as it is ... when a jury view premises as they are, without the slightest knowledge of what they were before, they may be influenced by the remark which was pressed upon me, but which I think is of no value whatever, namely, "Why, there are plenty of people in London who have not so much light as you have".'

There are other drawbacks, too, and we can be fairly sure he was alert to them, such as changing light conditions from day to day (note that he suggested the use of comparisons a year apart – implying the need to have at least similar weather for the experiment).

Accordingly, Dent & Co won their injunction.

Angus v Dalton/Dalton v Angus (1881)

This case has nothing whatever to do with light, but everything to do with rights to it. The reason for this apparent paradox is that it concerned the other most popular kind of negative easement, the right of support.

Consequently, the judges in the case kept alluding to analogous light cases. The full report of this case in the Queen's Bench Division and Court of Appeal runs to over 80 pages, from which the authors can pass on some selected gems.

The facts were very simple. Angus altered his premises 27 years before the events, so that his factory was more or less supported by a chimney stack which took the ends of some main girders. Dalton pulled down his property (somebody else's, actually: he was only the contractor) and carried out some excavation, leaving the stack standing on a pillar of clay, which soon collapsed, bringing the whole factory with it. All the argument was about whether the stack had acquired a right of support during those 27 years, as there was no way the servient owner could have stopped the acquisition, except by pulling down his own property and letting Angus fall down sooner. There was some subsidiary discussion as to whether client, contractor, or sub-contractor was liable, but that was very brief and need not concern us.

It seems that a judge heard the case with a jury, and then it passed to a bench of judges for the next stage. Lush, J heard the case originally, and then also delivered the first judgment of the Bench. He drew attention to the similarity of support and light, but pointed out that support was the more onerous, because of the difficulty of preventing the acquisition of rights.

While examining how rights were acquired, Lush, J remarked: 'I cannot help thinking that the revolting fiction of a lost grant may now be discarded'. One hundred years later, his wish has still not been granted. Another point of discussion he referred to was the difference of opinion between the Exchequer Chamber (whoever they were) and the Court of Queen's Bench as to whether the Statute of Limitations ran from the time when the wrong was committed or the time the damage actually occurred. As we know, that one hasn't finally worked itself out yet, either.

Having examined all the cases, he decided that the factory was 'ancient', and found for the plaintiffs: that they had a right of support.

Cockburn, CJ gave the second judgment, and said that the case was of 'very great importance as regards the law of easements'. He was the historian of the party and, after also deploring the fiction of the lost grant, examined the way in which prescription had developed. Different rights were, apparently, referred back to different dates. Until 1235, most rights had to be shown to date from before 1100. By the Statute of Merton, 1235, writs of right (it goes without saying that neither John nor Lance understood half of this, but are just passing it on, undigested) were limited to the time of Henry II, 70 years previously; writs of mort d'ancestor were not to pass the last return of King John from Ireland, a period of 25 years; and writs of novel disseisin were not to pass the first voyage of the King into Gascony, 15 years before. In 1275, the Statute of Westminster fixed new periods of limitation. Writs of right were limited to the time of Richard I, 1189; novel disseisin stayed where it was in Gascony; but writs of mort d'ancestor, cosinage, of aiel, and of entry were limited to the coronation of Henry III, about 58 years.

As the authors previously surmised, nobody then thought it worthwhile changing the date of prescription, even when, in Henry VIII's time, some of the other dates were altered. James I's reign brought another statute affecting limitation for possessory action, and there the law stayed until the time of William IV, not one of England's most memorable Kings, and the *Prescription Act* 1832, which we all know and love. So much for history.

Cockburn, CJ and John had at least one thing in common: they both thought that the *Prescription Act* could have been better worded. Indeed, the Lord Chief Justice went so far as to describe it as 'this strange and perplexing statute', which always made John feel a lot better about his own difficulties with it. The LCJ thought, and John agreed, that it would have been much more helpful to have had a series of fixed periods of prescription, with no other claims to be allowed except on production of positive proof of title – presumably written. Farewell the lost grant and time immemorial. He concluded that, 'by this roundabout and ... somewhat clumsy contrivance [referring to the 1832 Act] ... twenty years' use or enjoyment was rendered a presumption juris et de jure'.

Anyway, after much citing of cases, he concluded that as Dalton (or rather, his client, the Commissioners of Works and Buildings) had never granted a right of support or assented to Angus's construction, the right was open to be rebutted, and he found for the defendants. Fortunately for us, Mellor, J concurred with the Lord Chief Justice in nine lines.

The case then went to the Court of Appeal. Thesiger, LJ (doubtless an ancestor of the famous representatives of the clan today also dwelt upon the fiction of the lost grant, though he was by no means as opposed to it as

some of his fellows. After examining the remarks of the
LCJ in the court below, in a sentence rife with double
negatives, he agreed that the right of support was a bit
different from all others, except perhaps light. Although
we are only in the middle of his judgment (after 13
pages), he then summed up the question and effectively
gave his decision:

> 'Can it properly be said, then, that the difficulty
> or practical impossibility of obstruction in the
> case of the easement of support for a building by
> soil is such as to place it at common law in an
> entirely different category from other easements,
> and to render it subject to any real legal
> distinctions? I think not.'

Having reviewed the authorities, Thesiger, LJ was
satisfied that, for over 100 years, the courts had been of
the opinion that a right of support could be achieved by
proof of uninterrupted enjoyment for 20 years.
Accordingly, he gave judgment for the plaintiffs, unless
the defendants wanted a new trial (another bit of old-
fashioned legal proceedings).

Cotton, LJ gave the next decision, and argued that 20
years' enjoyment did not raise an absolute right, but a
presumption which could still be defeated by such
matters as the incapability of the grantor. The fact that
there was no grant (which all admitted) did not defeat the
presumption. He pointed out that enjoyment still had to
be open. (You may be surprised that no one quoted *nec
vi, nec clam, nec precario* in so many words.) He was not
sure that the mode of enjoyment had been known to the
servient owners, and thought that Lush, J should have left
that matter to the jury. For that reason, he, too, thought

that the defendants could have a new trial – presumably on that point only, the Court of Appeal having laid down the law on the right of support.

Finally, Brett, LJ delivered his speech. He pointed out that, despite their differing views on the proper verdict, the Queen's Bench had agreed on a great deal: that the right to lateral support for buildings is not a right of property; it can exist as an easement; it can only have its origin in a grant; that it's not covered by the *Prescription Act*; and that 20 years' enjoyment after knowledge by the adjoining owner was enough to secure the right – in the absence of other defects in the right. This question of knowledge was knocked about a bit, and has come up in other cases, including light ones, where a greater than ordinary amount of right was being claimed. It was certainly discussed in *Allen v Greenwood*. The servient owner has to be aware of the right which is being relied on, and then it presumably comes under the general heading of *nec clam*.

Brett, LJ summed up the differences by saying that Lush, J thought that, as a matter of law, after 20 years' enjoyment without physical obstruction, the right could not be defeated by the absence of a grant, or lack of knowledge by the defendant, or mere verbal objection. The other judges thought that the 20 years was only prima facie evidence of a grant, but that if there was doubt about it, it should be left to the jury, while if there was certainly no grant, judgment should be for the defendants.

He dismissed the claim, still being run by Angus's side, that support was a natural right in property – which would have given them a win by a knockout. In dealing with the next question, he pointed out that if a man erected a house with windows on the very extremity of his land, he needed no grant to do so. He only needed a grant if he wanted those windows to remain unobstructed. (At this point – in 1881 – he quotes *Gale on Easements*.) By 20 years of imposing this additional burden on next-door's land, he can achieve this putative grant, and the case with support is like unto it. The additional burden of the weight of the house prescribes for its right over time, so that on the day the house is built, only the land on which it stands has a right of support, whereas when it has been up for 20 years, the house itself is entitled to support. He agreed with all the points on which the Queen's Bench were agreed, and then turned to the points on which they differed.

Lush, J, in the opinion of Brett, LJ, went too far in his 'bold step' of holding that 20 years' enjoyment in itself confers a right. The jury should be allowed to find whether there was a grant – lost or otherwise. Brett seized on Lush's use of the words 'revolting fiction' to support the view that there must be a matter for the jury to decide. Use from 'time immemorial' means that a jury must find for prescription; use for a lesser length of time is only evidence on which they can make their own decision.

Brett, LJ reiterated all the points on which he and the Queen's Bench were agreed, and then held, for himself: that if there was no evidence led about the impossibility of the existence of a grant, the jury had to be directed to find a lost grant; if there was doubt as to the notice to the adjacent owner or the existence of a grant, it should be a matter for the jury; and if there was not sufficient evidence of the building having existed for 20 years, or if

there was positive evidence that there was no grant, then
the defendant was entitled to win. On the evidence, there
was no grant, therefore he would uphold the Queen's
Bench.

Three-all, therefore, after the most exhaustive
examination of the law, but the plaintiffs were left in
possession of the field – unless the defendants chose to
opt for a new trial.

So, there we are. An enormous commentary on a case
which has limited relevance to the matter in hand, but
which always intrigued John – and many others in this
field.

Shelfer v City of London Electric Lighting Company (1895)

This case also, of cardinal importance in dealing with
rights of light, had nothing to do with light at all. In fact,
the Lighting Company had caused damage by excavation
for the foundations of their plant, and were continuing to
cause annoyance by vibration and noise from it.
However, nuisance is nuisance, and the law is the same
when considering whether to grant an injunction or to
award damages in lieu. Mr Justice Kekewich (he who had
been junior counsel in Dent's case?) had awarded
damages, and the plaintiff appealed.

A substantial part of the case in the Chancery Court was
concerned with whether the Lighting Company were
exempt from an action because of their statutory position
(but this need not detain us). Having held that the
defendants could be – and were – liable, Kekewich, J
found that they had damaged the plaintiffs' premises so

as to make them less comfortable, but that the profits of Shelfer's business had not been interfered with, and that there would be great inconvenience if the defendants' business was stopped – among 1,500 or so buildings which they were supplying with electricity were the Bank of England, the Mansion House and the Guildhall. Accordingly, damages were a fair compensation, and no injunction ought to be granted.

In the Court of Appeal Lord Halsbury gave the first judgment. He was of the opinion that, without *Lord Cairns' Act* (*The Chancery Amendment Act* 1858), there would definitely have been an injunction. That Act, however, had changed the legal position, and the question was: to what extent? In his view, the well-settled principles indicated that an injunction was still appropriate in the present case, as otherwise a body such as the Lighting Company could force a neighbour to sell his rights.

Lindley, LJ, in giving the second judgment, instanced *Imperial Gas Light and Coke Co v Broadbent*, 1859, where the Lord Chancellor had said that damages 'cannot sufficiently indemnify the party who is injured', which made an injunction obviously necessary. It made no difference, in Lindley's view, whether the defendants were doing work of benefit to the public, and his only doubt about the effect of *Lord Cairns' Act* was whether it applied in *quia timet* actions. (That doubt no longer exists: see *Lyme Squash* below.) It was clear that the Act did not intend to turn the Court of Chancery into 'a tribunal for legalising wrongful acts'. He was of the opinion that damages should only be awarded instead of an injunction under 'very exceptional circumstances'. 'I will not attempt', he added, 'to specify them or to lay down rules for the exercise of judicial discretion'. A. L. Smith, LJ, as we shall see, was less hesitant about doing so.

In the third judgment, A. L. Smith was quite certain that jurisdiction existed to award damages or an injunction. The difficult question was: which? In answering his own question he made several very important observations, from which we can extract the following quotations.

> 'Many judges have stated, and I emphatically agree with them, that a person by committing a wrongful act ... is not thereby entitled to ask the Court to sanction his doing so by purchasing his neighbour's rights, by assessing damages in that behalf, leaving his neighbour with the nuisance, or his lights dimmed, as the case may be ...'

> 'In my opinion, it may be stated as a good working rule that –

> (1) If the injury to the plaintiff's legal rights is small,
> (2) And is one which is capable of being estimated in money,
> (3) And is one which can be adequately compensated by a small money payment,
> (4) And the case is one in which it would be oppressive to the defendant to grant an injunction:

> then damages in substitution for an injunction may be given.'

> 'There may also be cases in which ... the defendant by ... for instance, hurrying up his buildings ... has disentitled himself from asking that damages may be assessed in substitution for an injunction ...'

'An injury to … light to a window in a cottage
represented by £15 might well be held to be not
small … whereas a similar injury to a … large
building represented by ten times that amount
might be held to be inconsiderable. Each case
must be decided upon its own facts; but to escape
the rule it must be brought within the exception.'

It is clear not only that A. L. Smith had rights of light
well in mind, but also that he regarded an injunction as
being very much the normal remedy, and damages the
exception. Shelfer's case, in his judgment, was clearly not
a case for damages, but for an injunction to restrain the
continuance of the existing nuisance.

Whatever may be the practice today in commercial cases,
even when quite large injuries are in issue, the law is
perfectly clear, as was to be firmly reiterated in *Pugh v
Howells*, 1984 (see below). If his easement is threatened,
a man's basic right is to an injunction.

Colls v Home and Colonial Stores (1904)

The case is put this way because Colls brought the action
in the House of Lords, but he was the original defendant,
having sought to put up a building in Worship Street,
with the Home and Colonial Stores objecting. The High
Court had rejected the claim, but the Court of Appeal
had granted a mandatory injunction to pull the premises
down. Colls appealed against this to the Lords, who
unanimously upheld the appeal.

The Lord Chancellor, Lord Halsbury, gave the first
judgment, and quoted approvingly *Yates v Jack*, 1866, in
which Lord Cranworth said that the right was to 'the

enjoyment of the light without reference to the purposes for which it has been used', and also Malins, V-C, in *Lanfranchi v Mackenzie*, 1867, when he held that a person could not, even by using the dominant premises for 20 years for some special purpose requiring an extraordinary amount of light, acquire a right to some extra degree of light. (But see *Allen v Greenwood*, a bad decision in the authors' opinion, later.)

Another matter touched on was the question of alterations and their effect on the easement. The Lord Chancellor agreed that the non-user of a prescriptive right to light, or its partial use, did not detract from the right, but he felt that it was wholly unreasonable if a dominant owner could alter his building so as to impose an instant new burden upon his servient neighbour.

The main question to which Lord Halsbury addressed himself was whether the diminution of light suffered by the Home and Colonial justified the award of an injunction. The facts were that the room complained of was a long, deep one, with no windows at the rear, so that even a very moderately sized building opposite was bound to affect the penetration of light to the back of the room, although a normal sized and shaped room might have been unaffected. Relying on the finding of fact by the High Court judge that the building's effect on the light did not amount to a nuisance, he reversed the Court of Appeal's finding in law that the change was injunctable.

Lord Macnaghten, giving the second judgment, considered whether the law had been changed, except as to the period of enjoyment necessary to prove a right, by the *Prescription Act* 1832, and cited with approval judgments both before and after the passing of the Act which said, respectively: that it was necessary to 'distinguish between a partial inconvenience and a real injury to the plaintiff in the enjoyment of the premises'; and that for it to be actionable, the diminution had to be one which made the premises 'to a sensible degree less fit for the purposes of business or occupation'. He was of the opinion that the test was unchanged.

A most interesting observation he made was that instead of viewing the premises, a judge might well rely on the report of a competent surveyor appointed by the court. There is still a great deal of merit in this suggestion. It is very rarely that competent rights of light consultants disagree as to the facts of an injury: cross-examination is usually (but not always) directed at their opinion of the severity of the effect. Instead of wasting two chaps' time in court on a largely futile exercise, why not return the expert witness to his original function, that of assisting the court; let him report the facts and let the lawyers argue about the effect.

In his opinion, Lord Davey, with whom Lord Robertson agreed, also held that the test of nuisance was unchanged by the *Prescription Act*, and remarked that the purpose for which the dominant owner had thought fit to use the light did not affect the question. Lacking the Waldram diagram, which was not invented till later, he thought it perfectly proper for surveyors to employ the 45° rule as a good working guide, even if it was not a rule of law. (As we have the Waldram diagram, this is no longer true of the 45° rule, but the principle that a method which surveyors find to be of good practical assistance in determining the effect should be accepted, must still, surely, apply.)

Lord Lindley felt that it was unreasonable to allow no change in a dominant owner's light, or nothing would ever get built. He touched on the relevance of light from other directions, and thought that it should be disregarded if it could be legally interrupted. But it is his closing paragraph which, in many ways, is most interesting. He regretted the lack of a definite rule applicable to all cases, and said:

> 'First, there is the uncertainty as to what amount of obstruction constitutes an actionable nuisance; and, secondly, there is the uncertainty as to whether the proper remedy is an injunction or damages.'

It couldn't have been better put.

The next sentence is slightly more contentious:

> 'But, notwithstanding these elements of uncertainty, the good sense of judges and juries may be relied upon for adequately protecting rights to light on the one hand, and freedom from unnecessary burdens on the other.'

If anyone has to have faith in the law it ought to be the House of Lords, but if the lower courts are infallible, why do we need the higher ones?

Smith v Evangelization Society (Incorporated) Trust (1932)

A lot of what had been said in *Colls* was reiterated in this case, with some useful additions. Additions are what caused the problems, as well. An open space had gradually been walled and roofed, and skylights were put in and taken out again. In 1931, the defendants blotted out the light to a replacement eastern window. The celebrated Percy Waldram gave evidence for the plaintiff.

The whole case really turned on the skylights. If they had not been removed by the plaintiff, they would have provided enough light for the area which lost light through the obstructed window. The plaintiff argued that light from above was quite different, and ought not to be taken into account. The judge disagreed, and the plaintiff appealed.

The Master of the Rolls agreed with the judge's findings, quoted extensively from *Colls*, and rejected the appeal. Lord Hanworth said that you had to look at the premises at the start of the prescriptive period, and that the dominant owner was not entitled to claim an increasing use over the 20 years.

In the second judgment, Lawrence, LJ said that skylight was not analogous with reflected light, but was as good as, if not better than, side light. Romer, LJ, too, quoted from *Colls*, and pointed out that to lose light is not actionable in itself. Both judges therefore agreed with the Master of the Rolls in dismissing the appeal.

As skylights are very difficult to obstruct, and can light a large area, you should always keep your eyes open for them in areas where they might be relevant.

Sheffield Masonic v Sheffield Corporation (1939)

This is really the key case on light from alternative sources. Sheffield Masonic Hall had windows facing north and east, all of which were ancient, and Sheffield

Corporation began building a substantial art gallery and library to the north, which would obstruct the light to those windows. The Corporation argued that this didn't matter, provided that the eastern windows, which faced an open space, behind which was a low building, continued to provide enough light to the function room for ordinary purposes.

Maugham, J, in the Chancery Division, reviewed the arguments of the defendants, which could be summarised as 'first come, first served'. They should be allowed to build, they said, throwing the whole burden on to the eastern windows, and if someone came along later wanting to develop the open space, that was the later comers' hard luck. The judge felt that this gave rise to injustice, and that both servient owners would be placed under an uncertain obligation to the dominant owner. John always thought he was wrong in this, because to take the facts as you find them when you begin work on site is much easier than hypothesising about what might be built in front of the alternative windows.

However, the judge went on to take the other view:

> 'At the moment when the right is acquired by the plaintiff company in respect of both of the two windows on the north and the two windows on the east the nature of the restrictive obligation imposed upon people facing those two [did he mean four?] windows is that they will not so build as by their joint action to cause a nuisance to the plaintiff company.'

In other words, the Corporation could only build to a height which allowed a similar building to be erected on the land to the east which, when both buildings were considered jointly, would still allow enough light into all the windows taken together to be sufficient for the ordinary purposes of its user.

The judge then went on to cast doubt on the value of expert evidence, the Waldram diagram and the measurement of light at table height, saying that a building 10 feet away was much more injurious than one 60 feet away, even if they took away exactly the same amount of light. These are all propositions with which the authors would be prepared to argue.

For the rest, this case can almost be summed up in the words of Arthur Hugh Clough:

'And not by eastern windows only,
When daylight comes, comes in the light,
In front the sun climbs slow, how slowly,
But westward, look! the land is bright.'
(from *Say not the struggle nought availeth*)

Cory v CLRP (1954)

This case is an archetypal City (of London) rights of light case and Mr Justice Upjohn's judgment set out the legal considerations very clearly.

CLRP were about to redevelop 9–11 Billiter Square, when William Cory and Sons brought a *quia timet* action to stop them (that is to say, an action in which the plaintiffs 'fear lest' something might happen, rather than allege that it already has). It happened that the windows of the rooms of the major directors of the company on the first floor looked out at the site, together with those of several senior managers on the ground floor.

The judge said how well established the Waldram diagram was, and explained about the 'grumble line' – a term which is sometimes used for the 0.2% sky factor contour. He does not seem fully to have understood the conditions in which that 0.2% will have represented an actual one lumen contour, but he appreciated that the actual amount of light would vary with the seasons and the time of day. He also accepted the 50/50 rule (which is explained in Chapter 1), but warned that notions might change.

The figures put forward by the experts did not all agree, but the judge thought that the differences were not significant. Much more important was their agreement that loss of light to a room already ill lit was more serious than if the room began by being well lit. The rooms in question had previously been 50%, 45% and 40% well lit (or thereabouts) and it was proposed to reduce those areas by about 25%, 17% and 17% respectively. (The figures are given in the law report as percentages of the well-lit area: nowadays one normally talks of percentages of the whole room. We cannot be absolutely sure that the figures were not indeed of the latter kind.)

The judge then turned to considering whether damages or an injunction was the appropriate remedy. The argument had been put to him – as it nearly always is by defendants – that in reality the plaintiffs would suffer no loss, such was the demand for offices in that area. He rejected this approach, saying that the plaintiffs were not interested in dealing in offices, but in maintaining the light for the senior men of their organisation. There would be a real change in their conditions if the development were permitted and so, although the defendants might be placed in some difficulty by having to change their plans, get a new planning permission, and by the fact that they had already fabricated steel for the proposed building, he felt that an injunction was the proper remedy.

In passing, Upjohn, J referred to the movement of a partition which had occurred during the prescriptive period, and which had altered the prescriptive effect in two rooms.

He held, quoting *Colls*, that the right was to a shaft of light coming through the window, and that internal alterations, unless they were for extraordinary purposes, do not affect the dominant owner's right. John was not happy with this view, believing that it was too easy for the situation to be drastically altered by the dominant owner. He thought that a well-argued case, in which this was the main point, should result in the judgment that prescription must relate to one set of circumstances.

Ough v King (1967)

The issues in *Ough v King* can be very simply summarised. Mrs Ough claimed that her light had been injured. Bryan Anstey (John's illustrious father) gave evidence that just over 51% of the room remained well lit. The County Court judge visited the room on a grey afternoon in February and decided that the room was dark. As John always pointed out when writing or talking about this case, the Crystal Palace would have been dark in those circumstances. He therefore held that the light had been injured, and that the 50/50 rule which had been accepted in *Cory v CLRP* (see above) was not a rule of law (which we knew) and shouldn't therefore be slavishly adhered to (which may be regarded as unhelpful).

The Court of Appeal held that the judge was entitled to come to that decision. At least Diplock, LJ said that the 50/50 rule was still a convenient rule of thumb. Let us hope that the courts may continue to be all thumbs.

Metaxides v Adamson (1971)

The architects to the parties in this case had made what purported to be a party wall award, but as the houses were in Richmond, the 'award' had to be adopted by the principals by a deed of rectification. This gave the right to Mr Metaxides' predecessor in title to open certain windows. This was duly done by Mr Metaxides, and Mr Adamson then erected a trellis in front of the windows, and started growing pyracantha and wisteria up it.

Mr Metaxides sought a declaration that he was entitled to light through three windows, and an injunction restraining the plants. The judge held that the grant of the right to open the windows implied a grant of light to them and, accepting absolutely the evidence of Bryan Anstey, held that the kitchen had been seriously injured, the bedroom less so, and the lounge not at all.

Unfortunately, Mr Metaxides had been a bit slow in bringing his action, so that Mr Adamson had not been offered a chance to move his plants and establish them elsewhere. Accordingly, the judge decided against an injunction but ordered an enquiry as to damages.

Allen v Greenwood (1978)

This case was, in John's opinion, rightly decided in the lower court and wrongly reversed in the Court of Appeal. Over the years, the question of a right to an extraordinary amount of light had been much argued and, said Gale in the 13th edition of that work, 'finally decided in the negative in *Ambler v Gordon* 1905'. (Early in John's career he came across a case in which a family had matched fine silks in Soho for over 200 years, and yet were denied any greater than usual level of illumination by right of law.)

Mr Allen owned a house in Rochdale which had had a greenhouse since 1940. In 1974 Mr Greenwood proposed to erect an extension, to which Mr Allen objected, and later began to park a caravan immediately alongside the greenhouse. Then he began to erect a fence on the boundary, about 6 inches away from the greenhouse, and eventually extending to 18 inches above the eaves of the structure.

Vice-Chancellor Blackett-Ord found that, although the light had been affected, there was still plenty of light to do ordinary things, including reading a book. He remarked that 'there is no evidence that the owners of the servient tenement … knew the precise use which was being made' of the light in the greenhouse to grow tomato plants from seed. This 'precise' knowledge was a point discussed in *Dalton v Angus* (see above).

The Court of Appeal, having heard no argument to the contrary, held that a greenhouse was a building within the meaning of the *Prescription Act* 1832, and referred to an express decision to that effect in *Clifford v Holt*,

1899. The matter came down, therefore, to the question of whether the appellants could justify a claim to a 'specially high degree of light'. The respondents argued that it wasn't really the light which was making the difference, but the rays of the sun, which were a different matter entirely.

Goff, LJ started his examination of the law with *Colls v Home and Colonial Stores*, 1904 (see above), to establish the basic principle that enough light must be left for the ordinary purposes of a building. He was of the opinion that the ordinary purposes of a building which happened to be a greenhouse would require, and be entitled to, a greater amount of light. He also held that the servient owner would know the sort of uses to which greenhouses were put, and that he therefore did have sufficiently precise knowledge.

Goff, LJ's decision may be summarised as being to the effect that it was absurd if the plants had enough light to read their growing instructions, but not enough light to grow by. He dismissed the argument about the warmth of the sun, in the particular circumstances of this case, but said that at some future date, perhaps with reference to solar heating, it might be necessary to distinguish between daylight and sunlight. John agreed with that, but thought that those elements did get themselves confused on this occasion. The two other Lords of Appeal agreed with Goff, LJ without adding anything of any great importance.

It is notable that in this case, as in one or two others of importance, there does not seem to have been any expert evidence. John himself visited the site and, although he did not carry out a detailed inspection, came to the opinion that Mr Greenwood's house already overshadowed Mr Allen's greenhouse to some extent, and that the effect of the fence was not as great as believed by Mr Allen and the Court of Appeal. On a second visit, he found that Mr Greenwood, who refused to talk to him the first time, had parked his caravan alongside the greenhouse again.

Easthope v Gawthorpe (1983)

This is an unreported case which illustrates the application of the *Sheffield Masonic* principle, and also the dangers that may lurk in the wording of various covenants.

Mr Gawthorpe started to erect a substantial addition on the site of his garage, and Mr Easthope objected that it would darken the light to his living room, and to the bedroom above it. The expert consulted by Mr Gawthorpe was of the opinion that enough light would (or could, in the case of the bedroom, as there was a substantial item of furniture blocking the way) come to the rooms from other windows.

There was a complication in that there was a covenant in the deeds, saying that neither party (or any others on the estate) should do anything which might be or grow to be an annoyance to his neighbour. The lawyers for the defendant thought that if the injury was not an actionable one at common law, then this clause would not be infringed.

The matter was heard in the High Court before the judge, Finlay, J, who had been Counsel for King in *Ough* versus that gentleman. The expert for Mr Gawthorpe was terrified to discover that evidence for Mr Easthope was to be given by the man who had devised the daylight indicators, but fortunately the judge preferred the Waldram diagram method of calculation, saying that it was more suitable for intricate cases.

The plaintiffs naturally argued that the light from the alternative, smaller, window was not adequate and that, in any event, one should allow for a similar obstruction to its light. The judge held that the obstruction had to be a realistic possibility and that, as two long gardens and a road intervened between the window and any likely building, it could be considered to be free from risk of darkening. So John (that is to say, Mr Gawthorpe) thought he had won. But soft, what light through yonder window breaks? It is the covenant, and Mr Easthope is the beneficiary.

The judge decided that an injury need not be actionable for it to be an annoyance within the meaning of the deed, and therefore Mr Easthope was entitled to succeed. He didn't think, however, that the injury warranted an injunction, and so he awarded damages.

Richard Rogers, the architect, was less lucky with a similar covenant. There the judge awarded an injunction despite the fact that there was certainly no rights of light injury. He held that the mere presence of the proposed construction would be an annoyance to the neighbour. Fortunately, Mr Rogers' brilliant consultant was able to design a complicated structure, with planes meeting at all sorts of interesting angles, to such effect that it not only gave Mr Rogers all the space he needed, but will no doubt come in time to be considered a work of architectural genius and ascribed to the great man himself. (After all, that has already happened to some extent in respect of the chunk cut out of the southwest corner of the Lloyds building.)

It seemed to John a little harsh that, having succeeded in three-quarters of the case, Mr Gawthorpe should have to pay all the costs – but he did.

Pugh v Howells (1984)

In striking contrast to some people involved in leading cases, Miss Pugh was very hospitable when John asked if he might come and look at her house, but he was sorry to say that he was far from sure that she even suffered an actionable injury. If she did, however, then there is – paradoxically – no doubt that the Court of Appeal were correct in awarding her an injunction instead of damages. But let's look first at the facts of the case.

For many years, the possibility of an extension had been looming over the Pugh family; they had resisted it at every turn, with Miss Pugh taking the lead. Eventually, she noticed that Mr Howells had started taking down the lean-to extension at the rear of his house, which formed part of the same terrace as the Pughs' house. The latter already had a two-storey rear extension which had been constructed in about 1900. Miss Pugh's solicitors wrote and told the Howells that they would resist any building which affected the light to their rear room and kitchen. Over one Bank Holiday weekend, the defendants rushed up the extension to roof level.

Miss Pugh brought proceedings for an injunction in the County Court, and produced technical evidence which John regarded as worse than useless. No doubt her

178

consultants had done their best, but they relied on that most misleading of bases, light levels measured in lux or lumens within the room. On their first visit, they attempted to compare Miss Pugh's existing light with that of the next house up the hill, which happened to be affected by her existing extension. On their next visit, in completely different weather conditions, they measured the light now received in Miss Pugh's rooms after the Howells' extension was up. It is clear from their reports that the consultants recognised the deficiency of their system, but they still used it and attempted to extrapolate from their readings a scientific conclusion as to the effect on the Pughs' light.

The judge found that the Pughs' light had been injured, and awarded £500 in damages. At the time, the house was probably worth about £10,000. Miss Pugh, however, was a doughty fighter, and she did not want the money: she wanted her light. She consulted her barrister again, and he produced an excellent piece of reasoning as to why, given the judge's findings of fact, she should have obtained an injunction. Impressed by this, she bravely invested her savings in an appeal.

Counsel argued, and the Court of Appeal accepted, that all four tests laid down in *Shelfer* (see above) had to be passed before the court should exercise its discretion to award damages in lieu of an injunction. The judge had come to the conclusion that it was 'not a serious nuisance', and had paid no regard to the unhelpful behaviour of the defendants, both in dealing with correspondence and in hurrying up their building.

Waller, LJ, giving the first judgment, said that the judge had relied on reading a certain part of *Gale on*

Easements, and had said that although the Howells deserved no sympathy, he would only have ordered the work to be pulled down if he had thought that it was a serious nuisance. Waller pointed out that in his judgment on *Shelfer*, A. L. Smith had said that even if the four tests were passed, a defendant might by his conduct rule himself out of getting away with damages. Even though he, Waller, was not certain that the four tests had been passed in the present case, he would still have been reluctant to upset the judge's conclusion. However, as Howells' action clearly came within A. L. Smith's exceptions, he would allow the appeal and substitute an injunction.

In the second judgment, Fox, LJ opened by saying: 'This is a case in which there was a significant interference with the rights of light'. Later on, he stressed that the judge had not found that the injury was small, only that it was 'not a serious interference'. He, too, was mindful of the defendants' behaviour, and concurred in granting the injunction.

When John went to see the properties, the upper storey had been taken down, and only a single-storey extension – though much larger than the old lean-to – was in place. He therefore had to guess at the original extension. It was his impression that about 55% to 60% of the Pughs' two affected rooms would still have had 0.2% sky visibility. There is no doubt that they would have suffered loss, but not to the degree normally considered actionable by the courts. Miss Pugh was, he thought, very lucky in her choice of consultants, and, with more merit, her barrister.

The lesson of the case, however, does not of course lie in John's view of the facts, but the court's view of the law.

The *Shelfer* case was emphatically restated, and it was made very plain that reckless servient owners cannot expect any sympathy from the law. A man's basic right is still to an injunction: damages are the exception.

Lyme Valley Squash Club v Newcastle-under-Lyme BC (1984)

John disagreed with the decision in this case, and with the amount of damages awarded, but was told by the defendants' expert witness that while his grave doubts as to there actually being an injury were justified, they were wrong. In that expert's own words:

> 'the window head is set comparatively low and ... the internal depth of the room ... is unusually great in relation to ... window head height ... which results in an unusually low angle ... from the back of the room at working plane height to the window head.'

But all this will be meaningless to you, without having learned the basic facts.

A company which proposed to build a squash club bought a piece of land from the local authority, which retained land on three sides of the site. In the contract of sale was a condition that the purchaser was not to obtain any easements over the retained land which hindered its development; however, this clause was inadvertently omitted from the actual conveyance. It was accepted that the clause in the contract had not been deliberately inserted to allow for development: it was just in a standard form which happened to be used. At the time, it was expected that the area would be used as a car park.

At a later date, the council decided to allow some land to be developed for shopping, and the squash club objected that their light would be affected. Naturally, the council relied on the contract and the club on the conveyance. As it happened, the clubhouse had been at least partly built before the conveyance was executed, so that, if the words of the conveyance were held to govern, there would be an implied right to an easement to the windows. The judge held that, because no one gave any thought to the 'reservation' clause, it was right for him to go behind the contract, and find for the squash club.

In his judgment, Blackett-Ord V-C seized upon the words of Goff, CJ in *Allen v Greenwood* (see above) which, in John's opinion, had already overdeveloped the meaning of the judgment in *Colls* (again, see above) and said that a right to light was to that light required for the beneficial use of the building which received it. (As these cases follow each other, it would seem that the rule that there is 'no special right to light' is fast disappearing.) Although he was not impressed with the plaintiffs' valuer's evidence about the importance of light to a squash club lounge, the judge accepted that the light would be affected by the proposed building (which, as we explained at the outset, seemed unlikely to John, based on the facts he then knew) and that the plaintiffs ought to have damages, not an injunction, if the shop development went ahead.

Unfortunately, the defendants had offered to do some sort of landscaping for an area outside the windows, and were lured into costing that at about £10,000. The judge obviously thought that this was a useful figure, and so fixed upon it as the amount of damages. The order was made in a rather strange form, to the effect that if the defendants paid the money by a certain date, the injunction granted would not prevent them from building in accordance with the plans before the court.

Carr-Saunders v McNeil Associates (1986)

This case illustrates the limitations of the dictum that light receivable from other sources must be taken into account, and also the application of the principle of parasitical damages. In addition, it demonstrates the importance of speaking clearly when addressing the judge. Mr McNeil was a film producer, and urgent business had called him away. At one point, the judge asked why he wasn't present, and counsel replied that he was on location in Spain. The judge, mishearing the word as vacation, rather crossly asked what the defendant was thinking about, to go on holiday when an important case affecting him was being tried.

McNeil Associates and their architects had fallen into the common trap of believing that since they had planning permission and were really only bringing their building more or less into line with their neighbours, there was nothing to worry about. Unfortunately, they were building in Shorts Gardens, behind which lurks Neals Yard, the buildings of which were only a short distance away from the back of the development. Carr-Saunders objected that the light was being taken from the windows at the rear of his premises, which had been a warehouse, with no windows on the ground floor, open plan first and second floors with windows back and front, and a very high roof which Carr-Saunders had recently converted to provide living space for himself.

The first floor was still an open space, but the second floor was newly converted into small consulting rooms for an alternative medicine consortium. There was no doubt that the light to the two rooms at the rear had suffered, but McNeil's side (John among them) argued that the new conditions were not prescriptive, and that in the old open plan there would still have been 50% of the room well lit, as the windows on the opposite side were not likely to be obstructed and continued to provide plenty of light.

There were a number of subsidiary arguments, but the essence of the judge's decision on this point was that a reasonable man might want to divide a 20-foot-wide building into several rooms (even though Carr-Saunders had not done so when he occupied the second floor, nor in his new eyrie) and that the light from the opposite windows had never reached the areas which were now losing their light. John was never sure why this last point was relevant, as the ability to rely on other windows is surely bound to mean that some areas are lit by one window and some by another, and you must therefore consider the overall effect. However, there was no doubt that the cubicles had been seriously affected. The judge was saying, in effect, that you couldn't rely on windows 20 feet away to contribute to the lighting.

This brought those involved to the question of damages. There were two valuations before the judge: that of the plaintiff's architect, which did not follow any known precedents and reached the astonishing total of £24,000; and that of the defendant's expert, which had been prepared in accordance with John's principles, which amounted to £3,000.

The judge unhesitatingly accepted the figure of £3,000, but pointed out that damages were an equitable remedy, and that in deciding to forgo his right to an injunction, Mr Carr-Saunders would also have had in his mind the loss of sunlight (slight, but admitted by the defence) and the general deterioration in the ambience. For that reason he awarded a further £5,000, making £8,000 in all.

It would be dangerous to try to take a general rule from this case, but a rule of thumb multiplier of two and a half times the 'book' damages to forgo a possible injunction can sometimes be helpfully used. The authors have known cases, however, where one and a half was a better figure, and others where two and a half was laughed at for its inadequacy.

Deakins v Hookings (1993)

The really extraordinary thing about this case is that a pulling down injunction was awarded eight years after the offending construction was built. Although Miss Deakins objected as soon as she knew of the proposals, various legal delays meant that the case only came to court after a considerable lapse of time.

The building just round the corner from Miss Deakins' house, over which some of the light came to the rear living room in which she spent most of her time, was considerably extended and raised. This reduced the area of the living room which was well lit at table height from 50% to 41%.

There was also a small loss in the kitchen, which was complicated by the fact that additional light was received through a sort of glass lean-to and a glazed kitchen door. The judge ruled that this was to be taken into account in assessing the effect on the light in the kitchen. The area thus remaining well lit was 57.4%, compared with 88% before. The judge held that this room was not actionably affected, which lends support (but no more) to the view that 55% may be the safe limit for domestic premises.

In deciding that a mandatory injunction should be awarded to Miss Deakins, the judge took into account that 'though the loss of light is limited in scope it is none the less of real significance to somebody who is to live in that room'. It therefore failed the *Shelfer* (see above) test of 'small'. Miss Deakins' early and repeated objections to the development also contributed to her success.

The auld widow woman

Not every leading case should be taken at its face value.

That distinguished rights of light expert, Bryan Anstey, was once consulted, through solicitors, by an Irish bank. He carefully examined the drawings of the bank's extension, and its relation to the premises next door, and came to the conclusion that there was no actionable injury to the dominant owner's light (and so reported). He was surprised, therefore, to be asked to come over to Ireland for the trial of the neighbour's action against the bank for loss of light, and begged to be excused. The solicitors, however, insisted and said that his presence would be a great comfort to the bank.

Came the day of the trial, and the plaintiff gave evidence, with much affecting (and unconvincing) detail, none of which seemed to have anything to do with John's father. At lunchtime, Bryan Anstey plaintively enquired if he could go home now, as there was obviously no need for his services. 'I'm afraid not', said the solicitor. 'She's an auld widow woman and the judge is wanting to give her something'.

After lunch, the distinguished consultant from England gave his evidence, proving beyond doubt that there was no injury to the light, and the judge gave his verdict: judgment for the widow, and damages of £50. 'I see you were right,' said Bryan, 'but how could a poor old widow woman take the financial risk of such an action at law?' 'Well, she's a good customer of the bank, and they were supporting her', replied the solicitor. 'Which bank?' John's father asked, although he had already guessed the answer. 'Why, our clients, of course.' 'And what made you so sure she would win?' was the next question. 'Well you see', came the answer, 'some while ago she brought an action for breach of promise in this very court, and the same judge awarded her £50 damages. Her wily adversary, to avoid paying the money, married her instead and shortly afterwards decamped, so she really got neither her husband nor her damages. Well, the judge was determined that someone was going to pay her £50, and it just turned out to be the bank.'

It can sometimes be advisable to know more than the mere words of a judgment before placing any great reliance on a precedent.

Bowring Services Ltd v Scottish Widows Fund & Life Assurance Society (1995)

This case is important in understanding the workings of the Light Obstruction Notice process, the difference between temporary and permanent Light Obstruction Notices and the importance of taking action – it used to be a writ, but it is now the issue of a claim form – within a year of the date of the relevant notice.

The Light Obstruction Notice was initially registered on the basis of a temporary certificate, which was to expire within four months unless a definitive certificate was lodged. The definitive certificate was issued a couple of months later.

Proceedings were commenced to challenge the Light Obstruction Notice a year from the date of the permanent certificate, but failed because the court found that the start date of the year during which an action had to be brought to challenge the Light Obstruction Notice under section 3 of the *Rights of Light Act* 1959 was the date of the registration based on the temporary certificate. The writ was therefore out of time and ineffective to assert a claim under section 3 of the *Prescription Act* 1832.

The case is useful in setting out the proper method of challenging certificates issued by the Land Tribunal. It was claimed that the registrar's decision to issue the temporary certificate was invalid, but the court dismissed the claim on the basis that in this instance the proper method of challenge was by judicial review rather than by civil action.

The case also went on to explore additional niceties such as lost modern grant and the Custom of London. The ruling was that an alternative claim based upon lost modern grant failed because the Custom of London applied in this case. Finally, a further alternative claim based on common law prescription (requiring proof of the apertures back to 1189) also failed because there was clear evidence that the claimant's building was not in existence before the 1960s.

Midtown Ltd v City of London Real Property Company Ltd (2005)

Midtown was the freeholder of 43 Fetter Lane and its lessee was a firm of solicitors, Kendall Freeman. The City of London Real Property (CLRP) Company Ltd (part of the Land Securities group of companies) was the owner and proposed developer of a large neighbouring tract of land opposite 43 Fetter Lane. A resolution to grant planning permission was dated April 2004 and by the time the case was heard in January 2005 the soft strip element of the demolition process had commenced and full demolition was imminent.

The applicant sought an injunction or, in the alternative damages in lieu. The hearing dealt with the injunction issue only, with damages, if appropriate, to be dealt with by a separate trial (originally set for January 2006, but eventually settled out of court in advance).

The case lead to the judge considering various interesting points relating to rights of light including potential use of section 237 of the *Town and Country Planning Act* 1990 and how the question of compensation is then addressed. However, there are parts of the judgment that have lead to considerable subsequent debate in rights of light circles that continue as we speak.

One of the key points relates to the relative importance the judge attached to the fact that Kendall Freeman relied upon artificial lighting in their perimeter offices throughout the year despite the fact that the technical evidence proved that a perfectly adequate amount of natural light had been available over the CLRP site. The judge decided that while this had no bearing upon whether the injury were actionable or not – in fact, the impact upon natural light was undoubtedly very significant and thus at least potentially injunctable – it was a relevant and potentially important factor in deciding whether an injunction were in fact the appropriate remedy.

It was not denied that Kendall Freeman were in the habit of employing artificial light throughout the year, but it is questionable whether that should be taken to mean that natural daylight is of limited consequence or importance. While Lance fully accepts that modern artificial lighting is a significant improvement upon past versions and it is possible to work without access to natural light, he is absolutely convinced that the overwhelming majority of office workers welcome access to natural light even if they enhance that light with artificial lighting as well. Why else, for example, would Lance himself very quickly claim an office with the best natural light available when he moved to his current premises?

In many instances office users turn on artificial lighting out of habit even when it is not needed. However, the benefits of natural light must be emphasised, not simply in terms of the quality of light it provides, but also because we like to see the sky. We like to be in contact with the outside world and as a matter of choice prefer that to sitting in the middle of an open plan office floor with our only view being of a neighbouring building through the bodies of other office workers lucky enough to be nearer to the windows.

Natural light is probably of less importance in an office situation than a residential equivalent. For that reason, Lance understands that a judge would be more inclined to award damages than an injunction in respect of an office building, but Lance does not believe the decision in the *Midtown* case should lead any developer to the conclusion that he no longer need concern himself with the risk of injunction when impacting to any material extent upon natural light to an office. As the judge in the *Midtown* case said, if one were to follow that argument to its logical conclusion there would never be a successful rights of light challenge, because however much light was lost one would argue that one could fill the gap with artificial light.

Another important factor is that the judge decided that Midtown was a property investment company and that its only real incentive or interest in the property was financial. Taking that on a stage further, he was inclined to the view that it was really only after money rather than preservation of its light. Whether the judge was right in his assessment one cannot be certain, but it does emphasise the fact that if you want to protect and preserve your light, it is unwise to express any willingness to accept a financial settlement.

In Lance's opinion, the overriding reason why the judge elected not to grant an injunction in this case was the fact that the CLRP proposal had been in the public domain, in one form or another, for a significant period of time. It was not therefore something which had been thrust upon Midtown or their tenants at the last minute, and the applicants' position was significantly prejudiced by the fact that they had failed, perhaps refused, to respond to various promptings on the subject from CLRP and their rights of light consultant.

Courts do take full account of the actions of the parties prior to the injunction proceedings and will want to be satisfied that the affected party has acted in a proper and diligent fashion. For that reason, rarely is it a good tactic to sit back and wait, hoping to pounce on the developer at a later and more critical stage in the hope of securing the best settlement possible. It might work, but it can backfire.

Further reading

Anstey, B. and Chavasse, M., *The Right to Light*, Estates Gazette Ltd

Anstey, J., *Anstey's Boundary Disputes*, (3rd edition, updated by David Powell), RICS Books, 2004

Anstey, J., *Anstey's Party Walls*, (3rd edition, updated by Graham North), RICS Books, 2005

Bickford-Smith, S. and Francis, A., *Rights of Light: The Modern Law*, Jordans, 2000

Parry's Valuation and Conversion Tables, a College of Estate Management book published by the Estates Gazette Ltd

Littlefair, P., 'Site Layout Planning for Daylight & Sunlight: A Guide to Good Practice', BRE Guide, 1991

CIBSE, *Applications manual: Window design*, Chartered Institution of Building Services Engineers, 1987

Gaunt, J. and Morgan, P., *Gale on the Law of Easements* (17th edition), Sweet & Maxwell, 2002

Index